AVIATION SUPPLIES & ACADEMICS, INC.
NEWCASTLE, WASHINGTON

Sarah R. Anderson
Leslie M. Martin
Paul R. Snyder

AVIATION
HIGH SCHOOL

Learn Science, Technology, Engineering,
and Math through an exciting introduction
to the aviation industry

STUDENT NOTEBOOK

Aviation High School Student Notebook: Learn Science, Technology, Engineering, and Math through an exciting introduction to the aviation industry
by Brittany D. Hagen, Sarah K. Anderson, Leslie M. Martin, and Paul R. Snyder

AVIATION SUPPLIES & ACADEMICS, INC.
7005 132nd Place SE
Newcastle, Washington 98059
asa@asa2fly.com | 425-235-1500 | asa2fly.com

ASA-AVHS-SN
ISBN 978-1-61954-932-6

Additional formats available:
eBook PDF   ISBN 978-1-61954-935-7
eBook EPUB   ISBN 978-1-61954-933-3
eBundle   ISBN 978-1-61954-936-4 (print + eBook PDF download code)

Printed in the United States of America
2025   2024   2023   2022   2021   9 8 7 6 5 4 3 2 1

Cover images—Top: iStock.com/yongyuan. Bottom row (left to right): iStock.com/Jetlinerimages; iStock.com/Jetlinerimages; Pixabay; iStock.com/Dushlik; Mr. teerapon tiuekhom/Shutterstock.com.

Charts and other excerpts from the Piper Archer III PA-28-181 Pilot's Operating Handbook, report VB-1563 and VB-2749, are courtesy Piper Aircraft, Inc., and are for illustrative purposes only.

Library of Congress Cataloging-in-Publication Data:
Names: Anderson, Sarah K. (Sarah Katherine), author. | Martin, Leslie M., author. | Snyder, Paul R., author. | Hagen, Brittany D. (Brittany Dawn), author.
Title: Aviation high school student notebook : learn science, technology, engineering and math through an exciting introduction to the aviation industry / by Sarah K. Anderson, Leslie M. Martin, Paul R. Snyder, Dr., Brittany D. Hagen.
Description: Newcastle, Washington : Aviation Supplies & Academics, Inc., [2021] | Audience: Ages 14 - 18 | Audience: Grades 10-12
Identifiers: LCCN 2019055351 | ISBN 9781619549326 (trade paperback) | ISBN 9781619549333 (ebook) | ISBN 9781619549357 (pdf) | ISBN 9781619549364 (eBundle)
Subjects: LCSH: Aeronautics—Study and teaching (Secondary)—United States—Notebooks, sketchbooks, etc. | Airplanes—Piloting—Study and teaching (Secondary)—United States—Notebooks, sketchbooks, etc. | LCGFT: Notebooks.
Classification: LCC TL560.1 .A736 2021 | DDC 629.130071/273—dc23
LC record available at https://lccn.loc.gov/2019055351

CONTENTS

CHAPTER 1

AVIATION TRAINING REQUIREMENTS

CONTENTS

Check off each activity upon completion.

LESSON 1
PILOT CERTIFICATES AND RATINGS

ACTIVITY 1: Quote Review

Review the two quotes below. Think for one minute silently, and then share out loud with a partner. As a group, we will discuss your thoughts about your own motivations for studying aviation.

> Charles Lindbergh: "Science, freedom, beauty, adventure: what more could you ask of life?"[1]

> Wilbur Wright: "More than anything else the sensation is one of perfect peace mingled with an excitement that strains every nerve to the utmost, if you can conceive of such a combination."[2]

_____

_____

_____

_____

_____

_____

_____

_____

_____

_____

_____

_____

_____

_____

_____

_____

_____

_____

1   Charles A. Lindbergh, *The Spirit of St. Louis* (New York: Scribner, 2003), 261. First edition published 1953.
2   Dave English, *The Air Up There: More Great Quotations on Flight* (New York: McGraw-Hill, 2003).

ACTIVITY 2: Types of Pilot Certificates and Ratings

Rank the following pilot certificates in order from 1 to 6 based on how much training is required to obtain the certificates (1 = least amount of training, 6 = most amount of training).

Certificates and Ratings	Group Ranking	Reasons	Class Ranking	Evidence/Grounds from Interactive Lecture	Actual Ranking
Private					
Sport					
Student					
Commercial					
Airline Transport					
Flight Instructor					

ACTIVITY 3: Student versus Private Pilot Questions

Use your current FAR/AIM or **eCFR.gov** and the information presented in class to answer the following questions.

1. What is the difference between a student pilot and a private pilot? (Reference §61.89)

   _____

   _____

2. Can you as a student pilot fly from the United States to Canada? (Reference §61.89)

   _____

3. What is the minimum flight visibility that a student pilot can fly in during the day? At night? (Reference §61.89)

   _____

4. You see a break in the clouds up ahead. As a student pilot, can you legally fly through that opening and continue your flight above the clouds? (Reference §61.89)

   _____

5. Your relative really wants to go fly with you. Can you as a student pilot take your relative flying with you? (Reference §61.89)

   _____

6. You want to take an airplane from Grand Forks, ND, to Fargo, ND (68 NM away) to go to a baseball game. Can you, a student pilot, fly there by yourself? Why or why not? (Reference §61.93)

   _____

   _____

   _____

7. You want to fly to an airport located within the lateral limits of Class B airspace on your solo cross country during your private pilot training. What would your instructor have to do to allow you to take this flight? (Reference §61.95)

   _____

   _____

8. How old do you have to be to get your private pilot's license? (Reference §61.103)

   _____

9. 14 CFR §61.103 states that you must pass a practical test. What two parts does this test include? (Reference §61.103)

_____

10. How much total flight time is required to become a private pilot? (Reference §61.109)

_____

    a. Of that total, at least 20 hours is required to be with _____. This must include:

        i. 3 hours of _____

        ii. 3 hours of _____

        iii. 3 hours of _____

    b. This must include at least 10 hours of _____

        i. 5 hours of this must be _____

11. Can you as a private pilot get paid for flying someone around? (Reference §61.113)

_____

12. List 3 of the things that a private pilot can do. (Reference §61.113)

    1. _____

    2. _____

    3. _____

13. What are some of the ground and flight requirements to get a private pilot certificate?

_____

_____

_____

_____

_____

_____

_____

_____

_____

_____

_____

_____

14. What are the hourly requirements to get a private pilot certificate?

_____

_____

_____

_____

_____

_____

_____

_____

15. What are some places that you can go to get your private pilot's license?

_____

_____

_____

16. How much do these places typically charge for aircraft rental?

_____

_____

17. How much do these places typically charge for flight instructors per hour?

_____

_____

LESSON 2

TRAINING PROGRAMS

ACTIVITY 1: Top 10 Biggest Flight School Scams Recording List

1. _____
2. _____
3. _____
4. _____
5. _____
6. _____
7. _____
8. _____
9. _____
10. _____

ACTIVITY 2: Flight Training Worksheet

Directions: Research three places that conduct flight training in your area. Complete the required information to help you reach your aviation career goals. Your facilitator will complete the first example with the class.

EXAMPLE 1	
Name of Business	
Location	
What types of aircraft do they have?	
How much do they charge for ground instruction (CFI rate)?	
How much do they charge per hour for flight instruction?	

EXAMPLE 2	
Name of Business	
Location	
What types of aircraft do they have?	
How much do they charge for ground instruction (CFI rate)?	
How much do they charge per hour for flight instruction?	

EXAMPLE 3	
Name of Business	
Location	
What types of aircraft do they have?	
How much do they charge for ground instruction (CFI rate)?	
How much do they charge per hour for flight instruction?	

ACTIVITY 3: Final Thoughts Reflection

Summarize your research by completing the following statement.

I would choose _____ [enter flight training center name] because:

1. _____

2. _____

3. _____

LESSON 3

AVIATION MEDICALS

ACTIVITY 1: IMSAFE Checklist

	Area of Fitness to Fly	Question	Self-Evaluation
I			
M			
S			
A			
F			
E			

Are you safe to fly? Explain why you made this determination.

_____

_____

_____

_____

_____

_____

_____

_____

_____

ACTIVITY 2: Inquiry Question

Discuss the following question with a partner and record your response below.

> "How could the requirement of medicals affect the aviation industry both positively and negatively?

_____

_____

_____

_____

_____

_____

_____

_____

_____

_____

ACTIVITY 3: Aviation Medicals Graphic Organizer

Complete the chart on the next page by referencing 14 CFR §61.23 (Medical certificates: Requirements and duration) and then answer the comprehension questions that follow in Activity 4.

Use copies of the FAR/AIM manual or access the regulations online (eCFR.gov). Information can also be accessed through aviation organizations such as: American Association of Airport Executives (AAAE), Aircraft Owners and Pilots Association (AOPA), Women in Aviation International (WAI), The Ninety-Nines Inc., University Aviation Association (UAA), National Air Traffic Controllers Association (NATCA), Civil Air Patrol (CAP), Association for Unmanned Vehicle Systems International (AUVSI), and Experimental Aircraft Association (EAA).

Details and Requirements	Medical Certificate			
	Class I	Class II	Class III	UAV
Types of pilot				
Privileges				
Duration				
Distant vision				
Intermediate vision (distance of 32 in.)				
Near vision (distance of 16 in.)				
Color vision				
Hearing				
Blood pressure				
EKG (electrocardiogram)				
ENT (ear, nose, throat)				

ACTIVITY 4: Aviation Medicals Comprehension Questions

1. What are the privileges of a First-Class Airman Medical Certificate?

   _____

   _____

2. What are the privileges of a Second-Class Airman Medical Certificate?

   _____

   _____

3. What are the privileges of a Third-Class Airman Medical Certificate?

   _____

   _____

4. Where would you go to receive an Aviation Medical?

   _____

   _____

5. What would be a reason why your aviation medical would be revoked?

   _____

   _____

6. What is an aviation medical certificate?

   _____

   _____

   _____

   _____

7. Who must hold an aviation medical certificate?

   _____

   _____

   _____

8. What medical conditions does the FAA consider disqualifying?

   _____

   _____

   _____

   _____

   _____

9. What are the minimum and maximum ages for obtaining a medical certificate?

_____

_____

_____

10. Can I get my student pilot certificate at the same time I take my initial flight physical?

_____

11. Am I prohibited from exercising the privileges of my pilot certificate during medical deficiency?

_____

_____

12. Is a pilot required to report to the FAA that he or she has undergone LASIK or other laser eye surgery to correct vision?

_____

13. Can I appeal if my application for medical certification is denied?

_____

_____

14. How can I contact the FAA about my medical certificate?

_____

_____

15. I lost my medical certificate; how can I obtain a copy?

_____

_____

LESSON 4

AVIATION ORGANIZATIONS

ACTIVITY 1: List of Aviation Organizations

1. _____

2. _____

3. _____

4. _____

5. _____

6. _____

7. _____

8. _____

9. _____

10. _____

ACTIVITY 2: Professional Aviation Organization Research

With your group, research the professional aviation organization assigned by your teacher. Answer the following questions.

Name of organization _____

1. What is the impact of this aviation organization on the industry?

   _____

   _____

   _____

   _____

   _____

   _____

   _____

   _____

   _____

2. What are three reasons why you would join this organization?

   - _____

   - _____

   - _____

3. How much does it cost to join this organization?

   _____

4. What are the requirements to join this organization?

   _____

   _____

   _____

   _____

ACTIVITY 3: Persuasive Argument Exercise

Goal: Your task is to persuade airport personnel (your instructor and other teachers) to join your aviation organization.

Role: You are representatives from the aviation organization (e.g., president, CEO, government affairs, marketing, public relations, programing, pilot consultant).

Audience: You need to convince the airport director, the airport manager, and the air traffic controller to join your organization at the optimal membership level.

Situation: For some time, the key airport personnel have been discussing the ways they remain current in their professions and access aviation services. The airport director would like everyone to join AOPA, but the airport manager thinks it's a better idea for everyone to join the Civil Air Patrol. Additionally, the air traffic controller has suggested that EAA should also be considered. It is important for everyone to have the same membership to ensure consistency in benefits for all employees and pilots.

Product: A five-minute presentation to the class and airport personnel.

Standards and Criteria for Success:

Trait #1	Incorporates information from the organization	33%
Trait #2	Includes at least 3 persuasive reasons for joining	33%
Trait #3	Five-minute presentation offers a persuasive argument, involves all group members	33%

LESSON 5

REVIEW: AVIATION TRAINING REQUIREMENTS

ACTIVITY 1: Note-Taking Graphic Organizer

Know Well	Need to Review	Don't Know/Review More

LESSON 6
CHAPTER 1 EXAM

ACTIVITY 1: Writing Prompt

After reading the article provided by your facilitator, write a short paragraph responding to the prompt, "Explain why the Boeing 747 has run into problems recently and what it means about the aircraft." Use at least two details from the article to support your response.

_____

_____

_____

_____

_____

_____

_____

_____

_____

_____

_____

_____

_____

_____

_____

_____

_____

_____

_____

CHAPTER 2

AIRCRAFT BASICS

CONTENTS

Check off each activity upon completion.

LESSON 1

PARTS OF AN AIRPLANE

ACTIVITY 1: Parts of an Airplane Pre-Test

Complete the Parts of an Airplane Pre-Test found below. This test will not be graded, but will be used to gauge what you know about the parts of an airplane.

1. What is a fuselage?

   _____

   _____

   _____

   a. What material is it made out of?

      _____

      _____

2. What is an airfoil?

   _____

   _____

   _____

3. What are flaps?

   _____

   _____

   _____

4. What are ailerons?

   _____

   _____

   _____

5. What is an empennage?

_____

_____

_____

   a. What is a stabilizer and what is its function?

   _____

   _____

   _____

   _____

   b. What is a stabilator and what is its function?

   _____

   _____

   _____

   c. What is an elevator and what is its function?

   _____

   _____

   _____

6. What does trim do?

_____

_____

_____

7. What is the purpose of landing gear?

_____

_____

8. What are the two different types of landing gear configurations?

_____

_____

9. How do you control the aircraft movement while on the ground (i.e., what makes the aircraft turn left while taxiing)?

_____

10. What is the powerplant?

_____

_____

   a. Besides turning the propeller, what else does the powerplant do?

_____

_____

11. Label the components of the aircraft in the drawing below.

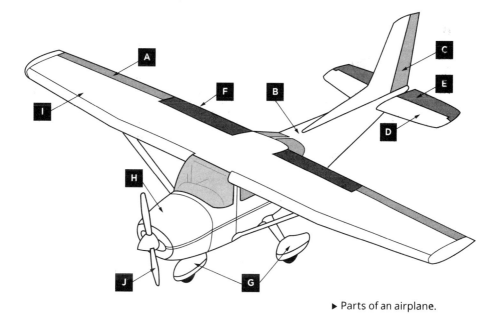

▶ Parts of an airplane.

A _____ F _____

B _____ G _____

C _____ H _____

D _____ I _____

E _____ J _____

ACTIVITY 2: Note-Taking Organizer for Parts of an Airplane

TOPIC (Questions, Key Points)	NOTES

SUMMARY

ACTIVITY 3: Parts of an Airplane Post-Lesson Test

Complete the Parts of an Airplane Post-Lesson Test below. These are the same questions you completed in the Pre-Test at the beginning of Lesson 1 and will help you assess what you have learned during this lesson.

1. What is a fuselage?

   _____

   _____

   _____

   a. What material is it made out of?

      _____

      _____

2. What is an airfoil?

   _____

   _____

   _____

3. What are flaps?

   _____

   _____

   _____

   _____

4. What are ailerons?

   _____

   _____

   _____

   _____

5. What is an empennage?

_____

_____

_____

   a. What is a stabilizer and what is its function?

      _____

      _____

      _____

      _____

   b. What is a stabilator and what is its function?

      _____

      _____

      _____

   c. What is an elevator and what is its function?

      _____

      _____

      _____

6. What does trim do?

_____

_____

_____

7. What is the purpose of landing gear?

_____

_____

8. What are the two different types of landing gear configurations?

_____

_____

9. How do you control the aircraft movement while on the ground (i.e., what makes the aircraft turn left while taxiing)?

_____

10. What is the powerplant?

_____

_____

   a. Besides turning the propeller, what else does the powerplant do?

   _____

   _____

11. Label the components of the aircraft in the drawing below.

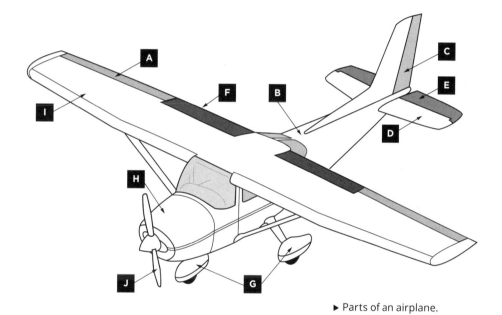

▶ Parts of an airplane.

A _____   F _____

B _____   G _____

C _____   H _____

D _____   I _____

E _____   J _____

LESSON 2

AIRCRAFT FLIGHT INSTRUMENTS

ACTIVITY 1: Aircraft Flight Instruments—Round Dial Cockpit

1. What are the flight instruments found in this round-dial cockpit? Fill in the names of the flight instruments next to the corresponding letters on the next page, and record 1–2 facts about each instrument, including what it tells the pilot.

(Images from FAA-H-8083-15B, FAA-H-8083-25B)

A. _____

    1. _____

    2. _____

B. _____

    1. _____

    2. _____

C. _____

    1. _____

    2. _____

D. _____

    1. _____

    2. _____

E. _____

    1. _____

    2. _____

F. _____

    1. _____

    2. _____

G. _____

    1. _____

    2. _____

2. Where are these instruments located in the cockpit?

_____

3. Why should pilots look at these instruments?

_____

_____

_____

_____

ACTIVITY 2: Aircraft Flight Instruments—Glass Cockpit

Label the glass cockpit flight instruments below.

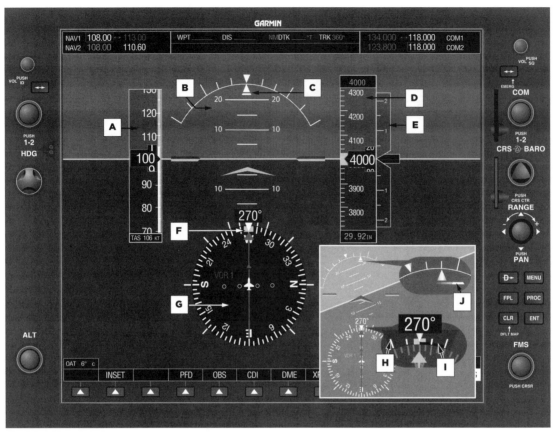

(FAA-H-8083-25B)

A. _____   F. _____

B. _____   G. _____

C. _____   H. _____

D. _____   I. _____

E. _____   J. _____

LESSON 3
FUNDAMENTAL MANEUVERS

ACTIVITY 1: Inquiry Research Project

Inquiry Chart (I-Chart) *(see next page)*

Of the questions listed below, select four questions or groups of questions that you would like to learn more about by researching with your partner. You and your partner must find at least three different sources to answer the inquiry questions. Use the inquiry chart on the next page to complete your research. Reference Chapter 3 in the *Airplane Flying Handbook* to answer your selection of the following questions. Be prepared to share your responses.

Fundamentals of Flight Inquiry Questions

1. What are the four fundamental maneuvers?

2. How should the pilot hold the controls?

3. What is meant by "feeling the airplane"?

4. What is attitude flying?

5. How much time should be spent looking inside versus looking outside the airplane?

6. What do the aircraft's flight instruments tell us?
   a. Airspeed indicator
   b. Attitude indicator
   c. Altimeter
   d. Vertical speed indicator
   e. Heading indicator
   f. Turn coordinator
   g. Magnetic compass

7. Straight-and-Level Flight:
   a. What instruments will tell us that the aircraft is level at 3,000 feet, on a heading of 350 degrees and at 110 knots?
   b. By looking outside, what are some ways in which the pilot can tell if the aircraft is straight and level?

(continued on page 35)

Inquiry Chart (I-Chart): Fundamentals of Flight

Chosen question:	Question 1	Question 2	Question 3	Question 4	Other interesting facts	New questions
Source 1						
Source 2						
Source 3						
Summary						

8. Level Turns:

    a. What instruments will tell us that the aircraft is level at 3,000 feet, turning from 350 to 090 degrees heading, at 110 knots?

    b. By looking outside while in flight, what are some ways in which we can tell if the aircraft is in a level turn?

    c. How does a constant airspeed impact the turn radius and rate?

    d. How does a constant angle of bank impact the turn radius and turn rate?

9. Climb:

    a. What instruments will tell us that the aircraft is climbing from 3,000 to 4,000 feet, on a heading of 350 degrees and at 110 knots?

    b. By looking outside, what are some ways in which we can tell if the aircraft is in a climb?

10. Descent:

    a. What instruments will tell us that the aircraft is descending from 4,000 to 3,000 feet, on a heading of 350 degrees and at 110 knots?

    b. By looking outside, what are some ways in which we can tell if the aircraft is in a descent?

LESSON 4
NORMAL TAKEOFFS AND LANDINGS

ACTIVITY 1: Pre-Lesson Question

How do you perform a normal takeoff in a small general aviation aircraft such as a Cessna 172 or Piper Cherokee? Record your answer in the space below.

_____

_____

_____

_____

_____

ACTIVITY 2: Normal Landings Outline

1. Final Approach:

   a. The _____ axis of the airplane should be aligned with the centerline of the runway.

   b. Slight adjustments in pitch and power may be necessary to _____

   _____

   c. Why is trim important?

   _____

   _____

   d. What part of the runway should the airplane land on?

   _____

   e. How are the four forces of flight related in a descent on final?

   _____

   _____

   _____

   f. How does wind impact the glide distance?

   _____

g. Why should a pilot never try to stretch a glide by applying only back pressure?

_____

_____

h. What effect do flaps have on a final approach?

_____

_____

i. What is downwash?

_____

_____

j. What is ballooning?

_____

_____

k. Where should we focus, on nearby objects or ones that are farther away?

_____

l. What are the hazards of focusing too far away? Too close?

_____

_____

m. When should a roundout be started?

_____

n. Back pressure should be _____ during a roundout.

o. Power is normally where during this phase?

_____

p. Why are visual cues important during a flare?

_____

_____

2. Touchdown:
    a. The airplane should never be flown on the runway with _____ speed.

3. After Landing Roll:

    a. Is the landing complete here? Why or why not?

_____

_____

    b. What is a ground loop?

_____

_____

_____

    c. How should we use our brakes?

_____

_____

    d. What do we use our yoke for on the ground?

_____

_____

ACTIVITY 3: Post-Lesson Question

How do you perform a normal takeoff in a small general aviation aircraft such as a Cessna 172 or Piper Archer? Record your answer in the space below.

_____

_____

_____

_____

_____

_____

_____

_____

_____

_____

_____

_____

_____

LESSON 5

TRAFFIC PATTERNS

ACTIVITY 1: Traffic Patterns Outline

Complete the following guided notes as your facilitator leads a discussion on approaches and landings.

Part 1

1. Standard versus non-standard turns

   _____

   _____

2. Traffic pattern altitude

   a. Non-published

   _____

   b. Published

   _____

Part 2

3. Look up _____ airport in the online *Chart Supplement*.

   a. Draw the runway diagram or layout.

b. What are the directions for each of the traffic patterns for each runway?

_____

_____

_____

_____

c. What is the traffic pattern altitude?

_____

_____

Part 3

4. Legs of a traffic pattern. List what the leg is and what the pilot and aircraft should be doing on each leg.

a. Upwind leg

_____

_____

_____

_____

b. Crosswind leg

_____

_____

_____

_____

c. Downwind leg

_____

_____

_____

_____

d. Base leg

_____

_____

_____

_____

e. Final leg

_____

_____

_____

_____

5. How does each of the following impact the legs of a traffic pattern?
    a. Strong wind

_____

_____

_____

    b. Light wind

_____

_____

_____

    c. We need to be angled sufficiently into the wind to prevent _____.

    d. When should you plan to turn to the next leg of the pattern?

_____

_____

_____

    e. Bank angles should not exceed _____. Why?

_____

_____

_____

_____

LESSON 6

HELICOPTER BASICS

ACTIVITY 1: Helicopter Questions

Follow your facilitator's directions on how to apply your knowledge to answer the following questions.

1. List one way in which a helicopter is like a fixed-wing aircraft such as a Cessna 172 or Piper Archer.

   _____

   _____

2. List one way in which a helicopter is different than a fixed-wing aircraft such as a Cessna 172 or Piper Archer.

   _____

   _____

3. What does the collective do?

   _____

   _____

4. What does the throttle do?

   _____

   _____

5. What does the cyclic do?

   _____

   _____

6. If I have a private pilot airplane pilot's license, can I fly a helicopter? Why or Why not?

   _____

   _____

LESSON 7

REVIEW: AIRCRAFT BASICS

ACTIVITY 1: Chapter Review Notes

_____

_____

_____

_____

_____

_____

_____

_____

_____

_____

_____

_____

_____

_____

_____

_____

_____

_____

_____

_____

_____

_____

_____

LESSON 8
CHAPTER 2 EXAM

ACTIVITY 1: Current Event Article

Article Response

Summarize the main point of the article:

_____

_____

_____

_____

_____

Select at least two of the inquiry questions listed below and answer them in the space provided. (Circle the questions you choose to answer.)

_____

_____

_____

_____

_____

_____

_____

_____

_____

_____

_____

_____

1. How does this article relate to the key concepts and big ideas we have studied this year, or to big ideas from your other classes?

2. What did you learn from the article that you did not previously know? What additional questions do you now have about the topic?

3. Identify a problem that needs to be solved within the situation presented in the article..

4. What is your opinion of the issue being discussed in the article? Do you agree/disagree with the writer/creator of this news item? Why or why not?

5. How could the knowledge you gained from the event be used in one or more of the professions with the aviation industry?

6. What are some questions you still have regarding this topic?

Write two questions you still have about this current event that were generated because you read the article.

_____

_____

_____

_____

_____

_____

_____

_____

_____

RESPONSE RUBRIC

	Exceeds Expectation (4)	Proficient (3)	Partially Proficient (2)	Novice (1)	Non-Performance (0)
Summary	Information is clearly summarized and demonstrates understanding of the topic. Includes strong supporting details addressing the who, what, where, when, why, and how questions.	Information from source is summarized and general comprehension is demonstrated. Includes supporting details addressing the who, what, where, when, why, and how questions.	Summary may be unclear, incomplete, copies the article, or is inaccurate. There is a need for more supporting details. Summary is only a few sentences.	Summary is vague, too much information was copied from the article, or important details are left out. Details or summary may be confusing.	No summary included.
Reflection	Student is able to relate article content to class material. Insightfully gives personal response with extremely strong thoughts and ideas. Two thoughtful, inquiry related questions are present.	General connection made between article and class material. Tells what their thoughts of the article are, with detail and description. Attempts to push thinking with some prompts. Two questions are submitted that relate to the field of aviation.	Simple or brief connection made between article and class material. Attempts to tell thoughts about the article. Lacks thoughtful ideas that relate to the article. Only one question present and/or are not applicable.	Attempt made to relate article content to class material. Response is inappropriate to the content of the article. Questions attempted.	No response written.
Conventions	Writer makes little or no errors in grammar or spelling that distract the reader from the content. Paragraphs contain sentences that are well-constructed. There are varied beginnings and rich and appropriate vocabulary.	Writer makes very few errors in grammar or spelling that distract the reader from the content. Most sentences are well-constructed with varied beginnings and vocabulary.	Writer makes some major errors in grammar or spelling. Some sentences may not be well-constructed. Similar words are used too often.	Writer makes many errors in grammar or spelling. Sentences lack structure and appear incomplete or are confusing.	No writing submitted or is illegible.

Comments

Total _____ / 12 pts

CHAPTER 3

AIRPORT OPERATIONS

CONTENTS

Check off each activity upon completion.

LESSON 1

INTRODUCTION TO AIRPORTS

ACTIVITY 1: Airport Operations Questions

▶ Airports (clockwise from top left): Alor Island Airport (Mali),[1] Lihue Airport,[2] Palm Beach County Park Lantana Airport,[3] and Palm Springs International Airport.[4]

Review the pictures above. Your facilitator will ask you to record your answers to the following questions to spark conversation about airport operations:

- What is an airport? _____

_____

_____

- Why are they designed so differently? _____

_____

_____

1   Photo by Ruddy Karundeng, https://commons.wikimedia.org/wiki/File:Aerial_of_Alor_Island_(Mali)_Airport.jpg.
2   Photo by Polihale at English Wikipedia (https://commons.wikimedia.org/wiki/File:Lihue-Airport-aerial.jpg), Wikimedia Commons, CC BY-SA 3.0 (https://creativecommons.org/licenses/by-sa/3.0/deed.en).
3   https://commons.wikimedia.org/wiki/File:Palm_Beach_County_Park_Lantana_Airport_photo_D_Ramey_Logan.jpg from Wikimedia Commons, photo by D Ramey Logan (https://don.logan.com/), CC-BY-SA 4.0 (https://creativecommons.org/licenses/by-sa/4.0/deed.en).
4   https://commons.wikimedia.org/wiki/File:Palm_Springs_International_Airport_photo_D_Ramey_Logan.jpg from Wikimedia Commons, photo by D Ramey Logan (https://don.logan.com/), CC-BY-SA 4.0 (https://creativecommons.org/licenses/by-sa/4.0/deed.en).

- What kinds of jobs are at an airport? _____

  _____

  _____

  _____

- What does it take to get a million people off the ground and up in the air? _____

  _____

  _____

  _____

ACTIVITY 2: Video Guided Notes

Question	Answers from *City in the Sky*
What is an airport?	
Why are they designed so differently?	
What kinds of jobs are at an airport?	
What does it take to get a million people off the ground and up in the air?	

ACTIVITY 3: Summary Prompt

Explain how an airport facilitates social, economic, scientific, and/or cultural exchange/change? Provide a detailed example for each topic area.

Social:_____

_____

_____

_____

_____

_____

Economic:_____

_____

_____

_____

_____

_____

Scientific:_____

_____

_____

_____

_____

_____

Cultural: _____

_____

_____

_____

_____

_____

LESSON 2

AIRPORTS

ACTIVITY 1: PHAK Airport Operations Questions

Answer the following comprehension questions by reading Chapter 14 in the *Pilot's Handbook of Aeronautical Knowledge*. Questions followed by an asterisk (*) indicate that it is an application question and you will have to apply what you learned in the book to answer the question.

Runways

1. All airport signs and markings are the same at all airports. This is mandated by the _____

   _____.

2. Runway numbers are always _____ and painted _____.

3. The runway numbers represent the first two digits of the runway's actual three-digit

   _____ direction.

4. A runway pointed 156 degrees becomes *Runway* _____. *

5. If one end of the runway is numbered 22, the other end of the runway would be

   numbered _____. *

6. When your airplane is pointed down any runway, the airplane's magnetic compass

   should indicate approximately _____.

7. Which two flight instruments could you use to find the aircraft heading?

   _____   _____

8. How does one say, "Runway 35"? _____. *

9. How does one say, "Runway 04"? _____. *

10. In the space below, draw and label runways with these options: 04, 15, 22, and 33
    (assume the top of the paper is magnetic north).*

Runway Lighting

11. _____ lights border the edges of the runway.

12. The beginning of the runway has _____ threshold lights.

13. The far end of the runway has _____ lights.

14. One side the lights are green and the other side of that same light is _____.

    This is because a runway's threshold is the other runway's _____.

15. Some runways have _____ lighting with embedded lights running the entire length of the runway.

16. Some airports have sequenced flashing _____ lights at the end of the runway. These are called runway end identifier lights or REILs.

Taxiways

17. Are taxiways named with numbers or letters? _____

18. What kind of map would assist a pilot in understanding complicated taxi instructions given by the ATC controller? _____.

19. All taxiway markings are in what color? _____

20. Taxiways are identified by a _____ _____ line down the middle of the taxiway.

21. Yellow letters against a _____ background indicate the taxiway you are currently positioned on (taxiway position sign).

22. _____ letters against a yellow background indicate an upcoming taxiway (destination sign).

23. If the taxiway is equipped with lights along the edge, they would be omni-directional and _____ (insert color). Omni-directional means _____. *

24. Taxiway centerline lights are _____ in color.

25. The _____ _____ marking is identified by two dashed yellow lines and two solid yellow lines.

26. If you are approaching double solid lines, are you coming from the taxiway side or the runway side?

    _____.

27. Do you need a clearance to cross the double solid lines at a towered airport? _____

28. If you are approaching the double dashed lines, are you coming from the taxiway side or the runway side?

   _____.

29. Do you need a clearance to cross the double dashed lines at a towered airport? _____

30. An aircraft is not clear of the runway until it has crossed over _____. *

31. What does CTAF stand for? _____ _____ _____ _____.

32. A runway boundary sign has _____ colored markings against a _____ colored background.

33. If you approach a sign that says "31 – 13", which runway would be to your left? * _____

34. Yellow chevrons prior to a runway indicate that the surface _____ (is / is not) for taxiing, takeoff, and landing.

35. White arrows pointing in one direction at one end of a runway designate a _____

   _____ which can be used for: (taxiing, takeoff, landing, emergency operations—circle all that apply).

Airport Beacons

36. Airports have rotating beacons to _____. They also indicate if the weather is less than VFR.

37. A civilian airport's beacon will consist of _____ and _____ colored alternating lights.

38. A military airport's beacon will consist of _____, _____,

   and _____ colored alternating lights.

39. Use the Twin Cities Sectional to see if Larimore Municipal Airport (2L1) in North Dakota has a rotating beacon. _____ *

40. Use the Twin Cities Sectional to see if Stephen Municipal Airport (D41) in Minnesota has a rotating beacon. _____ *

LESSON 3

MARKING AND SIGNAGE

ACTIVITY 1: Compass Rose Questions

Use the compass rose below to answer questions about cardinal directions and the directionality of classroom landmarks.

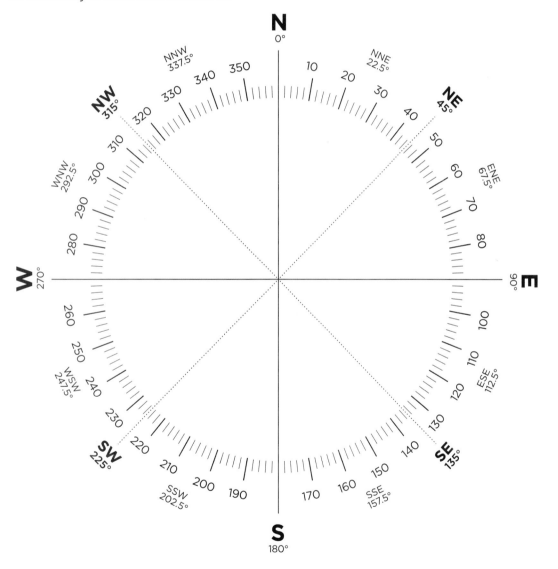

1. Where is the teacher's desk? _____

2. Where is the projector or smart board? _____

3. Where is the wall clock? _____

4. Where is the garbage can? _____

5. Where is the _____?

6. Where is the _____?

7. Where is the _____?

ACTIVITY 2: Airport Signs and Markings Graphic Organizer

Follow along with your facilitator's interactive lecture, using the graphic organizer below:

Type of Sign or Marking	Action or Purpose	Draw an Example
Runway Threshold		
Displaced Threshold		
Runway Safety Area		
Runway Holding Position Sign		
Runway Holding Position Marking		
Runway Designation Marking		
Temporarily Closed Runways and Taxiways		
Permanently Closed Runways and Taxiways		

Type of Sign or Marking	Action or Purpose	Draw an Example
No Entry		
Mandatory Instruction Signs		
Location Signs		
Direction Signs		
Destination Signs		
Information Signs		
Runway Distance Remaining		

ACTIVITY 3: Airport Diagrams

In the diagrams below, label the runways with the signs and markings indicated.

1. Draw and label the location of the following three different types of airport signs on the Aspen airport diagram shown on page 59:

   - Mandatory instruction sign

   - Runway distance remaining sign

   - Location sign.

2. Identify and label one possible location of each of the six different types of location signs on the airport diagram for Daniel K Inouye INTL (HNL) (PHNL) shown on page 60:

   1. Mandatory instruction sign

   2. Location sign

   3. Direction sign

   4. Destination sign

   5. Information sign

   6. Runway distance remaining sign

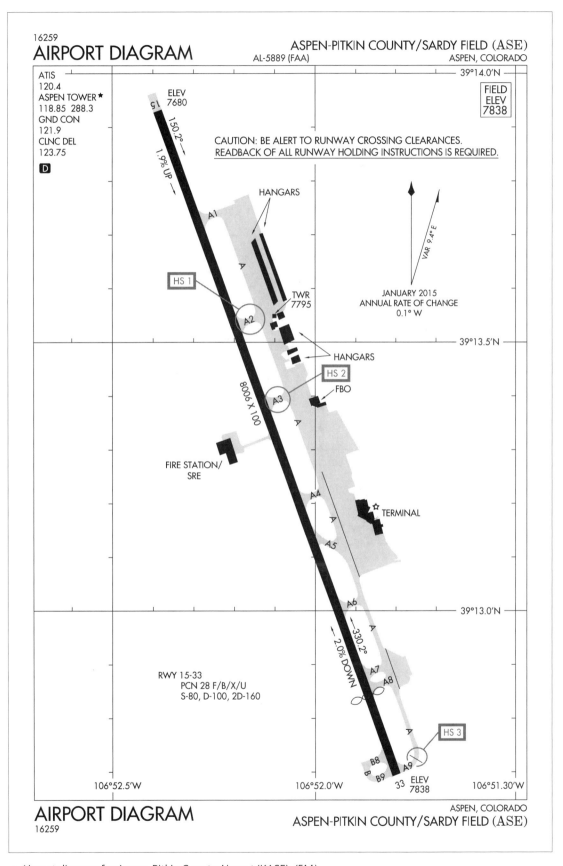

AIRPORT DIAGRAM

AL-5889 (FAA)

ASPEN-PITKIN COUNTY/SARDY FIELD (ASE)

ASPEN, COLORADO

ATIS
120.4
ASPEN TOWER ★
118.85 288.3
GND CON
121.9
CLNC DEL
123.75

D

39°14.0'N

FIELD
ELEV
7838

ELEV
7680

15

150.2°

1.9% UP

CAUTION: BE ALERT TO RUNWAY CROSSING CLEARANCES.
READBACK OF ALL RUNWAY HOLDING INSTRUCTIONS IS REQUIRED.

VAR 9.4° E

JANUARY 2015
ANNUAL RATE OF CHANGE
0.1° W

HANGARS

A1

A

HS 1

A2

TWR
7795

39°13.5'N

HANGARS

HS 2

A3

FBO

8006 X 100

A

FIRE STATION/
SRE

A4

A

TERMINAL

A5

A6

39°13.0'N

A

330.2°

2.0% DOWN

RWY 15-33
PCN 28 F/B/X/U
S-80, D-100, 2D-160

A7

A8

A

HS 3

B8

A9

B B9

33 ELEV
7838

106°52.5'W

106°52.0'W

106°51.30'W

AIRPORT DIAGRAM

16259

ASPEN, COLORADO
ASPEN-PITKIN COUNTY/SARDY FIELD (ASE)

▶ Airport diagram for Aspen-Pitkin County Airport (KASE). *(FAA)*

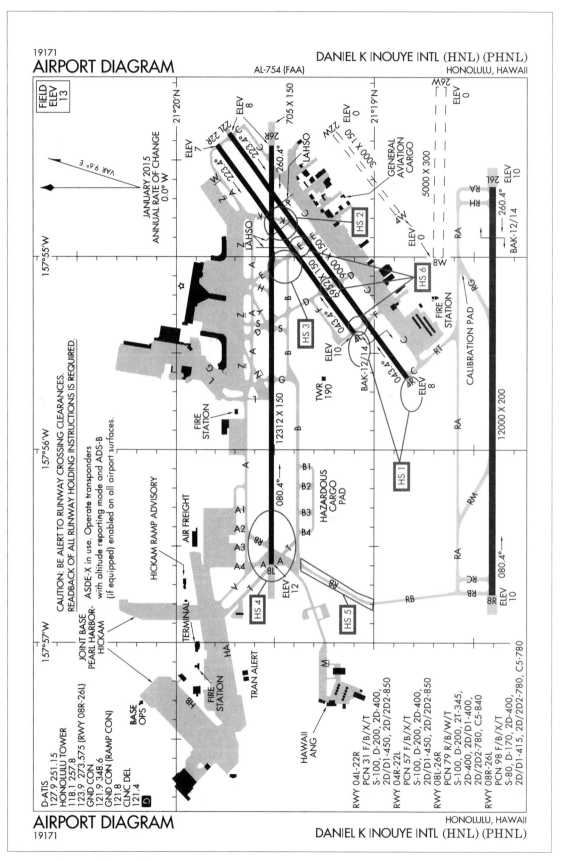

▶ Airport diagram for Daniel K. Inouye International Airport (PHNL) in Honolulu, Hawaii. *(FAA)*

CHAPTER 3 Lesson 3 / Student Notebook

ACTIVITY 4: Runway Layout Activity

1. Label each runway. Options are: 03, 08, 21, and 26.

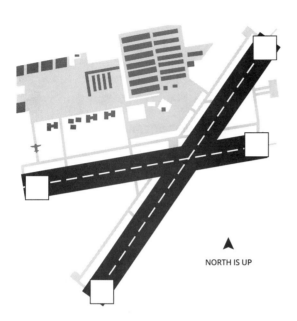

NORTH IS UP

2. Label each runway. Options are: 04L, 04R, 09, 14, 15L, 15R, 22L, 22R, 27, 32, 33L, 33R.

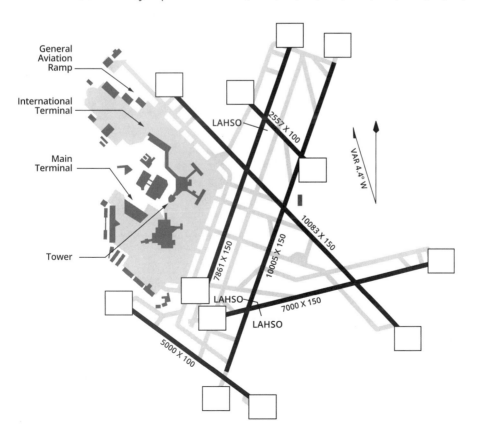

LESSON 4

AIRPORT LIGHTING

ACTIVITY 1: Airport Lighting Chart

Follow along with your facilitator's interactive lecture, using the graphic organizer below:

Type of Lighting	Purpose	Color
Airport Beacon		
Airport Beacon: Water Airport		
Airport Beacon: Heliport		
Airport Beacon: Military		
Approach Lighting System		
Visual Approach Slope Indicator (VASI)		
Precision Approach Path Indicator (PAPI)		
Runway End Identifier Lights (REIL)		
Runway Edge Lights		
In-Runway Lighting		
Taxiway Edge Lights		
Taxiway Centerline Lights		
Clearance Bar Lights		
Runway Guard Lights		
Stop Bar Lights		
Obstruction Lights		
New Lighting Technologies		

ACTIVITY 2: Chart Supplement Example

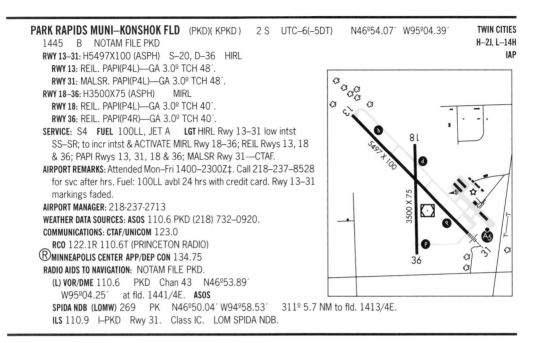

PARK RAPIDS MUNI–KONSHOK FLD (PKD)(KPKD)   2 S   UTC–6(–5DT)   N46°54.07′ W95°04.39′   **TWIN CITIES**
  1445   B   NOTAM FILE PKD   H–2J, L–14H
  RWY 13–31: H5497X100 (ASPH)   S–20, D–36   HIRL   **IAP**
    RWY 13: REIL. PAPI(P4L)—GA 3.0º TCH 48′.
    RWY 31: MALSR. PAPI(P4L)—GA 3.0º TCH 48′.
  RWY 18–36: H3500X75 (ASPH)   MIRL
    RWY 18: REIL. PAPI(P4L)—GA 3.0º TCH 40′.
    RWY 36: REIL. PAPI(P4R)—GA 3.0º TCH 40′.
  SERVICE: S4   FUEL 100LL, JET A   LGT HIRL Rwy 13–31 low intst
    SS–SR; to incr intst & ACTIVATE MIRL Rwy 18–36; REIL Rwys 13, 18
    & 36; PAPI Rwys 13, 31, 18 & 36; MALSR Rwy 31—CTAF.
  AIRPORT REMARKS: Attended Mon–Fri 1400–2300Z‡. Call 218–237–8528
    for svc after hrs. Fuel: 100LL avbl 24 hrs with credit card. Rwy 13–31
    markings faded.
  AIRPORT MANAGER: 218-237-2713
  WEATHER DATA SOURCES: ASOS 110.6 PKD (218) 732–0920.
  COMMUNICATIONS: CTAF/UNICOM 123.0
    RCO 122.1R 110.6T (PRINCETON RADIO)
  ®MINNEAPOLIS CENTER APP/DEP CON 134.75
  RADIO AIDS TO NAVIGATION: NOTAM FILE PKD.
    (L) VOR/DME 110.6   PKD   Chan 43   N46°53.89′
      W95°04.25′   at fld. 1441/4E.   ASOS
  SPIDA NDB (LOMW) 269   PK   N46°50.04′ W94°58.53′   311º 5.7 NM to fld. 1413/4E.
  ILS 110.9   I–PKD   Rwy 31.   Class IC.   LOM SPIDA NDB.

▶ Chart Supplement for Park Rapids, Minnesota (KPKD). *(FAA)*

Circle, highlight, or label the following information on the chart supplement above:

1. Frequency to activate pilot-controlled lighting

2. Intensity of pilot-controlled lighting

3. Does the airport have any visual slope indicators like a VASI or PAPI?

4. Does the airport have an approach lighting system?

5. Where is the airport beacon located?

ACTIVITY 3: Chart Supplement Research

Look up a local airport in the chart supplement to answer the following questions.

Name of airport _____

1. Does this airport have pilot-controlled lighting? _____

2. If so, what is the frequency to activate pilot-controlled lighting? _____

3. What is the intensity of pilot-controlled lighting? _____

4. Do any of the runways have in-runway lighting? _____

5. Does the airport have any visual slope indicators like a VASI or PAPI? _____

    a. If so, which one and where? _____

    _____

6. Does the airport have an approach lighting system? _____

    a. If so, which one and for which runways? _____

7. Where is the airport beacon located? _____

ACTIVITY 4: Chart Supplement Airport Homework

Answer the following questions while referencing the appropriate *Chart Supplement*.

Reference Anoka County Airport (KANE) in the North Central U.S. *Chart Supplement* for questions 1–4.

1. What is the field elevation? _____

2. What is the traffic pattern altitude? _____

3. What is runway 09-27 light intensity? _____

4. What is the frequency to turn on the lights? _____

Reference Brainerd Lakes Regional Airport (KBRD) in the North Central U.S. *Chart Supplement* for questions 5–9.

5. What is the field elevation? _____

6. What is the traffic pattern altitude? _____

7. What is runway 05-23 light intensity? _____

8. What is the frequency to turn on the lights? _____

9. Is runway 05 left or right traffic? _____

Reference West Fargo Municipal Airport (D54) in the North Central U.S. *Chart Supplement* for questions 10–17.

10. What is the field elevation for West Fargo, ND (D54)? _____

11. Runway 18 at D54 has what direction of traffic pattern?

    a. Standard

    b. Non-standard

12. Runway 36 at D54 has what direction of traffic pattern?

    a. Standard

    b. Non-standard

13. What is the width and length of runway 18-36? _____

14. What is the traffic pattern altitude? _____

15. What is the CTAF frequency? _____

16. What type of pilot-controlled lighting does runway 18 have? _____

17. How many clicks will turn on the lighting for runway 18? _____

LESSON 5

GUEST SPEAKER—OPERATIONS

ACTIVITY 1: Double Entry Notes

Name: _____   Date: _____

Guest Speaker: _____   Title: _____

From the speaker...	From my mind...

ACTIVITY 2: Inquiry Question

Summarize the connection of the guest speaker's presentation to at least one course inquiry question from the list below.

_____

_____

_____

_____

_____

_____

_____

_____

_____

_____

Inquiry Questions

1. How does this aviation topic facilitate social, economic, scientific, and/or cultural exchange/change?

2. What larger concept, issue, or problem underlies this topic in aviation?

3. What do you notice about how things work in this aviation topic?

4. What are some things we could not do without understanding this topic in aviation?

5. If we changed one thing about how this works, what do we think would happen?

6. How do small changes in aviation affect the larger system?

7. What is the impact of this part of aviation on society?

8. How does this part (e.g., ATC, airports, UAS, flight training, etc.) of the aviation industry affect the other parts?

9. What mistakes have been made in aviation? What did we learn from them? What changes were made?

10. What are current issues in aviation? What caused them? What is a viable solution? What would be consequences of the solution?

11. Can you suggest a different way of doing this in aviation?

12. What conclusions about this topic can be made?

13. What patterns can you see across topics in aviation?

14. What reasons might there be for these patterns?

15. How do you think technology might change how we do this in the future?

16. How will automation and/or autonomous operations change how this is accomplished in the future?

LESSONS 6 & 7

AIRPORT DESIGN PROJECT—INTRODUCTORY AND WORK DAYS

ACTIVITY 1: Building Hong Kong's Airport Notes

What are the reasons for a new airport?

_____

_____

_____

_____

_____

What are some of the challenges facing the engineers?

1. _____

_____

_____

2. _____

_____

_____

3. _____

_____

_____

What concerns still exist about the airport?

_____

_____

_____

_____

_____

ACTIVITY 2: Engineering Design Graphic

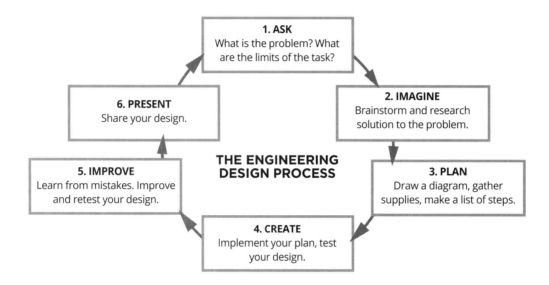

1. ASK
What is the problem? What are the limits of the task?

2. IMAGINE
Brainstorm and research solution to the problem.

3. PLAN
Draw a diagram, gather supplies, make a list of steps.

4. CREATE
Implement your plan, test your design.

5. IMPROVE
Learn from mistakes. Improve and retest your design.

6. PRESENT
Share your design.

THE ENGINEERING DESIGN PROCESS

ACTIVITY 3: Design Process Example Graphic Organizer

Follow along as your facilitator models how to complete the Design Process Graphic Organizer below.

THE DESIGN PROCESS EXAMPLE GRAPHIC ORGANIZER	
ASK	What is the problem? What do you already know? What are the limits or controls of the task?
IMAGINE	What are some solutions to the problem? Research. Brainstorm.
PLAN	Draw a diagram. What supplies will you need? Who will do the jobs? Make a list of the steps you will take.
CREATE	Follow your plan. Collaborate with your team. Work. Test your design.
IMPROVE	Learn from mistakes. Make your design better. Test it again and redesign.
PRESENT	Share your design.

ACTIVITY 4: Airport Design Project Assignment

Assignment Description

The purpose of this assignment is for your group to use the engineering design process and your knowledge of airports to design an airport of your own. You will create a large poster of your airport. To successfully complete this project, your group must follow these steps:

1. Collect necessary supplies (poster board, markers, computer/printer, etc.).

2. List your group members as assigned by your instructor:

   _____   _____   _____   _____

3. Pick a location for your airport: _____

4. Pick a name for your airport: _____

5. Select an identifier for your airport: _____

6. In the design of your airport, include these features:

   - One paved runway, correctly marked

   - One grass runway, correctly marked

   - Two major taxiways, two connections to the end of the runway, and one mid-point intersection with the runway, all correctly marked

   - All runways and taxiways must have signs at the intersections and the ends

   - Airport signage should be drawn at every intersection

   - Ramp with an FBO, correctly marked

   - Segmented wind circle, correctly marked

   - Green space (e.g., trees, grassland, landscape)

   - Runway End Identifier Lights (REILS)

   - Beacon on the field (what colors will your beacon be?)

7. Create a well-organized and accurate *Chart Supplement* insert for your airport, including the following elements:

   - Pilot-controlled lighting

   - CTAF frequency (what frequency will they be activated on? HIRL, MIRL or LIRL?)

   - Field elevation

   - Traffic pattern altitude

   - Runway dimensions (length and width)

   - Runway surface material

8. Present your airport designs to the class. Airport designs should be presented clearly and logically so the audience can follow your line of reasoning. While presenting, keep eye contact with the audience and speak in a clear, precise manner. Answer audience questions clearly and completely.

9. Use the following graphic organizer to plan your airport design and review the grading checklist to guide your successful completion of this project.

THE AIRPORT DESIGN PLANNING GUIDE

ASK	What is the problem? What do you already know? What are the limits or controls of the task?	
IMAGINE	What are some solutions to the problem? Research. Brainstorm.	
PLAN	Draw a diagram. What supplies will you need? Who will do the jobs? Make a list of the steps you will take.	
CREATE	Follow your plan. Collaborate with your team. Work. Test your design.	
IMPROVE	Learn from mistakes. Make your design better. Test it again and redesign.	
PRESENT	Share your design.	

AIRPORT DESIGN GRADING CHECKLIST

Group Members: _____

Engineering Design Process	Checklist	Comments
Ask: Carefully considers prior knowledge, limits, and controls that impact the project outcome.	/5	
Imagine: Generate and explore multiple ideas and options for airport design. Consideration is given to recent innovations and technological advances in aviation.	/5	
Plan: Critically evaluate each of the design requirements. Work to generate different design possibilities and keep record of plans and revisions.	/5	
Create: Creatively and responsibly uses materials and resources	/5	
Improve: Self-critique the prototype and analyze the design for accuracy and areas for improvement	/5	

Airport Design Requirements	Checklist	Comments
Location, name, and identifier (unique to location) of airport are clearly marked	/5	
1 paved runway identified and correctly marked	/5	
1 grass runway identified and correctly marked	/5	
2 major taxiways with two connections at the ends and one midpoint, correctly marked	/5	
Ramp with FBO correctly marked	/5	
Segmented circle correctly marked	/5	
Greenspace (e.g., trees/landscape)	/5	
Runway End Identifier Lights (REILS)	/5	
Airport beacon	/5	

Chart Supplement Insert Requirements	Checklist	Comments
Organization/accuracy	/5	
Pilot controlled lighting	/5	
CTAF frequency (HIRL, MIRL or LIRL)	/5	
Field elevation	/5	
Traffic pattern altitude	/5	
Runway dimensions	/5	
Runway surface	/5	

Presentation Requirements	Checklist	Comments
Explanation of airport design is presented clearly and logically so the audience can follow your line of reasoning.	/5	
While presenting, keep eye contact with the audience and speak in a clear, precise manner.	/5	
Answer audience questions accurately.	/5	
Total	/120	

SELF-EVALUATION RUBRIC

Student's name: _____   Date: _____

Project: _____   Average: _____ out of 4

KEY
1 = **Beginning**—experiences difficulty even with teacher prompting
2 = **Developing**—inconsistent and/or requires teacher prompting
3 = **Accomplished**—consistent with little or no teacher prompting
4 = **Exemplary**—consistent and independent

	Student Evaluation	Teacher Evaluation
Ask		
Carefully consider the investigation guidelines.		
Thoughtfully discuss multiple relevant and interesting questions for further exploration.		
Determine multiple team or individual goals in response to your questions.		
Imagine		
Without teacher guidance, generate and explore numerous ideas, responses, and solutions.		
Independently generate clever, unique, or unusual ideas.		
Work with teammates to imagine many different possible solutions to the team's questions and the design challenge.		
Independently perceive and accept the team's many differing positions and points of view.		
Plan		
Critically evaluate the purpose of every detail of the design.		
Keep detailed records and sketches of design possibilities, plans, and revisions.		
Conduct research and use prior knowledge as a foundation for prototype plans		
Create		
Persevere to create a functioning prototype.		
Creatively and responsibly use materials and resources.		
Improve		
Without teacher guidance, self-critique the prototype and analyze all design flaws.		
Suggest multiple solutions to problems, or multiple ways to improve the efficiency or quality of the prototype.		

LESSON 8

AIRPORT DESIGN PROJECT—PRESENTATIONS

ACTIVITY 1: Presentation Viewing Graphic Organizer

Directions: Watch each of your classmates' airport design presentations. Complete a graphic organizer for each presentation that you watch.

Presenters	
Location	
Name/Identifier	
Interesting highlights	
What makes this an effective airport design?	
Ranking	

Presenters	
Location	
Name/Identifier	
Interesting highlights	
What makes this an effective airport design?	
Ranking	

Presenters	
Location	
Name/Identifier	
Interesting highlights	
What makes this an effective airport design?	
Ranking	

Presenters	
Location	
Name/Identifier	
Interesting highlights	
What makes this an effective airport design?	
Ranking	

Presenters	
Location	
Name/Identifier	
Interesting highlights	
What makes this an effective airport design?	
Ranking	

Presenters	
Location	
Name/Identifier	
Interesting highlights	
What makes this an effective airport design?	
Ranking	

Presenters	
Location	
Name/Identifier	
Interesting highlights	
What makes this an effective airport design?	
Ranking	

Presenters	
Location	
Name/Identifier	
Interesting highlights	
What makes this an effective airport design?	
Ranking	

Presenters	
Location	
Name/Identifier	
Interesting highlights	
What makes this an effective airport design?	
Ranking	

Presenters	
Location	
Name/Identifier	
Interesting highlights	
What makes this an effective airport design?	
Ranking	

LESSON 9

AIRPORT OPERATIONS REVIEW STUDY GUIDE

ACTIVITY 1: Study Guide Questions

Directions: Record your initial answers to the study guide questions below. Do not use your prior assignments or the *Pilot's Handbook of Aeronautical Knowledge* until instructed to do so by the facilitator. You may need to reference your *Chart Supplement* to answer the following questions.

1. Draw and label the parts of a standard traffic pattern. Describe what you are expected to do on each leg.

2. In what direction are the turns made in a standard traffic pattern?

_____

3. If not stated in the *Chart Supplement*, how high above ground should you fly a traffic pattern?

_____

4. What does CTAF stand for?

_____

5. What is the field elevation for Jamestown Regional Airport, North Dakota (KJMS)?

_____

6. Runway 31 at KJMS has what direction of traffic pattern?

   a. Standard
   b. Non-Standard

7. What is the width and length of runway 31?

_____

8. What is the traffic pattern altitude for Jamestown, North Dakota (KJMS)?

_____

9. If the wind is coming from 180 degrees at 15 knots, which runway would you plan to land on at Jamestown, ND?

_____

10. What is the CTAF frequency for Jamestown, ND?

_____

11. How high above the traffic pattern altitude should you be when overflying the airport to check on the wind sock?

    a. 1,000 feet
    b. 500 feet

12. What type of pilot-controlled lighting does runway 31 have?

_____

_____

13. How many clicks will turn on the lighting for runway 31?

_____

14. What is a hold short position marking?

_____

_____

_____

15. Which side of the hold short position marking has a solid line and which side has a dashed line?

_____

_____

16. What aircraft activities are allowed on a displaced threshold?

_____

_____

17. What type of airport sign is yellow with black writing?

_____

_____

18. What type of airport sign is black with yellow writing?

_____

_____

19. What type of airport sign is red with white writing?

_____

_____

20. Why would an airport's rotating beacon be on during daylight hours?

_____

_____

21. What colors is a civilian land airport's rotating beacon?

_____

22. What colors are a military airport's rotating beacon?

_____

23. If you see a PAPI and it is 2 whites and 2 reds, what does that mean?

_____

_____

24. If you see a VASI and it is white over white, what does that mean?

_____

_____

25. What are REILS?

_____

    a. What color are they?

    _____

26. What color are taxiway edge lights?

_____

27. What color are runway edge lights?

_____

28. Do aircraft take off into the wind or with the wind?

_____

    a. Why?

    _____

    _____

29. Do aircraft land into the wind or with the wind?

_____

    a. Why?

    _____

    _____

30. Why is it so important to rotate at the proper speed on takeoff?

_____

_____

_____

_____

31. Why is it important to be on the correct final approach speed while landing?

_____

_____

_____

_____

32. What is V_X?

_____

_____

_____

_____

33. What is V_Y?

_____

_____

_____

_____

LESSON 10

REVIEW: AIRPORT OPERATIONS

ACTIVITY 1: Chapter Review Notes

_____
_____
_____
_____
_____
_____
_____
_____
_____
_____
_____
_____
_____
_____
_____
_____
_____
_____
_____
_____
_____
_____
_____

LESSON 11

CHAPTER 3 EXAM

ACTIVITY 1: Article Response and Rubric

Write a two-paragraph response that includes a summary and reflection on the prompts below:

"How does the importance of weight and balance technology in conducting safe and efficient flight impact aircraft passengers?"

"What is your opinion: Should passengers pay for two seats if they're overweight or naturally large or even be forced to sit in 'fat zones' so airlines can work out a more exact weight and balance of aircraft and in turn cut operating costs?"

The two-paragraph response will be graded using the rubric provided on the next page.

_____

_____

_____

_____

_____

_____

_____

_____

_____

_____

_____

_____

_____

_____

_____

_____

_____

_____

_____

RESPONSE RUBRIC

	Exceeds Expectation (4)	Proficient (3)	Partially Proficient (2)	Novice (1)	Non-Performance (0)
Summary	Information is clearly summarized and demonstrates understanding of the topic. Includes strong supporting details addressing the who, what, where, when, why, and how questions.	Information from source is summarized and general comprehension is demonstrated. Includes supporting details addressing the who, what, where, when, why, and how questions.	Summary may be unclear, incomplete, copies the article, or is inaccurate. There is a need for more supporting details. Summary is only a few sentences.	Summary is vague, too much information was copied from the article, or important details are left out. Details or summary may be confusing.	No summary included.
Reflection	Student is able to relate article content to class material. Insightfully gives personal response with extremely strong thoughts and ideas. Two thoughtful, inquiry related questions are present.	General connection made between article and class material. Tells what their thoughts of the article are, with detail and description. Attempts to push thinking with some prompts. Two questions are submitted that relate to the field of aviation.	Simple or brief connection made between article and class material. Attempts to tell thoughts about the article. Lacks thoughtful ideas that relate to the article. Only one question present and/or are not applicable.	Attempt made to relate article content to class material. Response is inappropriate to the content of the article. Questions attempted.	No response written.
Conventions	Writer makes little or no errors in grammar or spelling that distract the reader from the content. Paragraphs contain sentences that are well-constructed. There are varied beginnings and rich and appropriate vocabulary.	Writer makes very few errors in grammar or spelling that distract the reader from the content. Most sentences are well-constructed with varied beginnings and vocabulary.	Writer makes some major errors in grammar or spelling. Some sentences may not be well-constructed. Similar words are used too often.	Writer makes many errors in grammar or spelling. Sentences lack structure and appear incomplete or are confusing.	No writing submitted or is illegible.

Comments

Total

_____ / 12 pts

CHAPTER 4

WEIGHT & BALANCE AND PERFORMANCE

CONTENTS

Check off each activity upon completion.

LESSON 1

WEIGHT AND BALANCE INTRODUCTION

ACTIVITY 1: Comprehension Questions

Write down answers to the following questions presented in class.

1. Why do we compute weight and balance before every flight?

   _____

   _____

   _____

   _____

   _____

2. What do the Federal Aviation Regulations (14 CFR §91.103, **faa.gov**) say about weight and balance?

   _____

   _____

   _____

   _____

   _____

3. How do we figure out the aircraft's useful load?

   _____

   _____

   _____

4. Why might there be a difference between the maximum ramp weight and maximum takeoff weight?

   _____

   _____

   _____

   _____

   _____

ACTIVITY 2: Vocabulary Chart

Define the following terms as they are presented in class.

Term	Definition
Basic Empty Weight	
Standard Empty Weight	
Useful Load	
Payload	
Center of Gravity (CG)	
Datum	
Moment	
Maximum Ramp Weight	
Maximum Taxi Weight	
Maximum Takeoff Weight	
Maximum Landing Weight	

ACTIVITY 3: True or False Statements

True or False   Pilots should compute weight and balance before every flight.

True or False   An aircraft will have a shorter takeoff distance when it's heavily loaded than when it's lightly loaded.

True or False   A heavily loaded aircraft will have a shorter landing distance than if that same aircraft were lightly loaded.

True or False   For a pilot to compute takeoff and landing distances, the pilot must first compute the aircraft's weight.

True or False   A light aircraft will have reduced fuel economy (rate of fuel burned) as compared to a heavy aircraft.

True or False   The starting point for every weight and balance calculation is the standard empty weight.

LESSON 2

WEIGHT AND BALANCE COMPUTATION

ACTIVITY 1: Weight and Balance Reference Charts

Weight and Balance Loading Form

(From the Piper Archer III PA-28-181 POH. For example only; do not use for flight planning.)

SECTION 6
WEIGHT AND BALANCE   **PA-28-181, ARCHER III**

	Weight (Lbs)	Arm Aft Datum (Inches)	Moment (In-Lbs)
Basic Empty Weight			
Pilot and Front Passenger		80.5	
Passengers (Rear Seats)*		118.1	
Fuel (48 Gallon Maximum)		95.0	
Baggage (200 Lbs. Maximum)*		142.8	
Ramp Weight (2558 Lbs. Normal, 2138 Lbs. Utility Maximum)			
Fuel Allowance For Engine Start, Taxi and Run Up	-8	95.0	-760
Takeoff Weight (2550 Lbs. Normal, 2130 Lbs. Utility Maximum)			

Totals must be within approved weight and C.G. limits. It is the responsibility of the airplane owner and the pilot to ensure that the airplane is loaded properly. The Basic Empty Weight C.G. is noted on the Weight and Balance Data Form (Figure 6-5). If the airplane has been altered, refer to the Weight and Balance Record for this information.

*Utility Category Operation - No baggage or rear passengers allowed.

- Calculate the takeoff center of gravity.

_____

- Is the aircraft's takeoff CG within limits?

_____

- Calculate the following:

  Landing weight: _____

  Landing moment: _____

  Landing CG: _____

Weight vs. CG Envelope Chart

(From the Piper Archer III PA-28-181 POH. For example only; do not use for flight planning.)

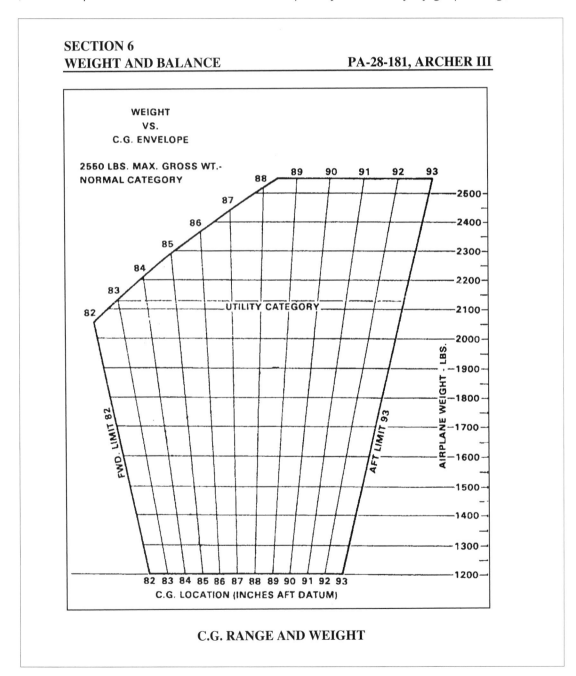

ACTIVITY 2: Weight and Balance Worksheet

Use this worksheet as directed by your facilitator.

	Weight	Arm	Moment
Basic Empty Weight (BEW)			
Pilot			
Front Passenger			
Rear Passengers			
Baggage			
Fuel			
Ramp Weight			
Run-up			
Takeoff Weight			

- Is the aircraft weight below the maximum takeoff weight?

  _____

- Is the aircraft's takeoff CG within limits?

  _____

NOTE: This worksheet is meant as a guide to calculate weight and balance. Always verify your actual weight and balance with the aircraft POH prior to each flight.

ACTIVITY 3: Weight and Balance Exercises

Weight and Balance Exercise 1

The aircraft you will be flying today has a BEW of 1,662.78 lbs and a moment of 146,840.14 in-lbs. You weigh 125 lbs. Your two friends are coming along for this flight and your friend who weighs 110 lbs wants to sit in the front. Your other friend is OK sitting in the back and he weighs 200 lbs. They are bringing a small bag that weighs 20 lbs. The plan is to go with full fuel (48 gallons). Complete this weight and balance problem.

	Weight	Arm	Moment
Basic Empty Weight (BEW)			
Pilot			
Front Passenger			
Rear Passengers			
Baggage			
Fuel			
Ramp Weight			
Run-up	−8	95	−760
Takeoff Weight			

Are you within limits?

_____

Why or why not?

_____

If not, what could you do to bring the aircraft back within limits?

_____

Weight and Balance Exercise 2

The aircraft you will be flying today has a BEW of 1,658.4 lbs and a moment of 146,361.59 in-lbs. You weigh 300 lbs. Your two friends are coming along for this flight and your friend who weighs 200 lbs wants to sit in the front. Your other friend is OK sitting in the back and she weighs 125 lbs. They are bringing a bag that weighs 50 lbs. The plan is to go with full fuel (48 gallons). Complete this weight and balance problem.

	Weight	Arm	Moment
Basic Empty Weight (BEW)			
Pilot			
Front Passenger			
Rear Passengers			
Baggage			
Fuel			
Ramp Weight			
Run-up	−8	95	−760
Takeoff Weight			

Are you within limits?

_____

Why or why not?

_____

If not, what could you do to bring the aircraft back within limits?

_____

Weight and Balance Exercise 3

The aircraft you will be flying today has a BEW of 1,661.40 lbs and a moment of 146,454.59 in-lbs. You weigh 125 lbs. Your three friends are coming along for this flight and your friend who weighs 125 lbs wants to sit in the front. Your other friends are OK sitting in the back and they weigh 200 lbs and 175 lbs. You also plan to bring a bag that weighs 50 lbs. Since you have three passengers, you decide to only fuel the aircraft with 30 gallons of fuel. Complete this weight and balance problem.

	Weight	Arm	Moment
Basic Empty Weight (BEW)			
Pilot			
Front Passenger			
Rear Passenger			
Rear Passenger			
Baggage			
Fuel			
Ramp Weight			
Run-up	−8	95	−760
Takeoff Weight			

Are you within limits?

_____

Why or why not?

_____

If not, what could you do to bring the aircraft back within limits?

_____

Weight and Balance Exercise 4

This is a blank worksheet that can be used for additional practice. Your facilitator will provide further directions.

	Weight	Arm	Moment
Basic Empty Weight (BEW)			
Pilot			
Front Passenger			
Rear Passengers			
Baggage			
Fuel			
Ramp Weight			
Run-up	−8	95	−760
Takeoff Weight			

Are you within limits?

_____

Why or why not?

_____

If not, what could you do to bring the aircraft back within limits?

_____

LESSON 3

CURRENT EVENT

ACTIVITY 1: Current Event Outline and Rubric

Article Title:_____

Source: _____ Date published:_____

Summarize the main point of the article:

_____

_____

_____

_____

_____

_____

Select at least two of the inquiry questions listed below and answer them in the space provided. (Circle the questions you choose to answer.)

_____

_____

_____

_____

_____

_____

_____

_____

_____

_____

_____

_____

_____

_____

_____

_____

_____

_____

_____

_____

_____

Inquiry Questions:

- How does this article relate to the key concepts and big ideas we have studied this year, or to big ideas from your other classes?

- What did you learn from the article that you did not previously know? What additional questions do you now have about the topic?

- Identify a problem that needs to be solved within this situation.

- What is your opinion of what you are reading and the issue being discussed? Do you agree/disagree with the writer/creator of this news item? Why or why not?

- How could the knowledge you gained from the event be used in your future aviation career?

- What are some questions you still have regarding this topic?

Write two questions you still have about this current event that were generated because you read the article.

_____

_____

_____

_____

_____

_____

_____

_____

CURRENT EVENTS RUBRIC

	Exceeds Expectation (4)	Proficient (3)	Partially Proficient (2)	Novice (1)	Non-Performance (0)
Article	Article is well-chosen given topic and inquiry questions from relevant website or news source. All the required information is cited clearly and correctly in MLA format. Article is handed in with the assignment.	Article is from relevant web source and related to aviation. The required citation information is complete. Article is handed in with the assignment.	Article may not be from relevant or appropriate source. The title, source, or one other piece of information may be missing from the citation. Article is handed in with the assignment.	Article may be inappropriate for course topics and important information about the article is missing.	No article submitted.
Summary	Information is clearly summarized and demonstrates understanding of the topic. Includes strong supporting details addressing the who, what, where, when, why or how questions.	Information from source is summarized and general comprehension is demonstrated. Includes supporting details addressing the who, what, where, when, why, or how questions.	Summary may be unclear, incomplete, copies the article, or is inaccurate. There is a need for more supporting details. Summary is only a few sentences.	Summary is vague, too much information was copied from the article or important details are left out. Details or summary may be confusing.	No summary included.
Response	Student is able to relate article content to class material. Insightfully gives personal response with extremely strong thoughts and ideas. Two thoughtful, inquiry related questions are present.	General connection made between article and class material. Tells what their thoughts of the article are, with detail and description. Attempts to push thinking with some prompts. Two questions are submitted that relate to the field of aviation.	Simple or brief connection made between article and class material. Attempts to tell thoughts about the article. Lacks thoughtful ideas that relate to the article. Only one question present and/or are not applicable.	Attempt made to relate article content to class material. Response is inappropriate to the content of the article. Questions attempted.	No response written.
Conventions	Writer makes little or no errors in grammar or spelling that distract the reader from the content. Paragraphs contain sentences that are well-constructed. There are varied beginnings and rich and appropriate vocabulary.	Writer makes very few errors in grammar or spelling that distract the reader from the content. Most sentences are well-constructed with varied beginnings and vocabulary.	Writer makes some major errors in grammar or spelling. Some sentences may not be well-constructed. Similar words are used too often.	Writer makes many errors in grammar or spelling. Sentences lack structure and appear incomplete or are confusing.	No writing submitted or is illegible.

Suggested grading conversion scale: A = 16-14   B = 13-10   C = 9-8   D = 7-4   F = 3-0

Comments

Total _____ / 16 pts

LESSON 4

PERFORMANCE INTRODUCTION

ACTIVITY 1: Factors that Affect Performance Chart

Factors that Affect Performance	How the Factor Affects Performance

ACTIVITY 2: Takeoff Charts

(The following charts are from the Piper Archer III PA-28-181 POH. For example only; do not use for flight planning.)

Flaps Up Takeoff Performance Chart

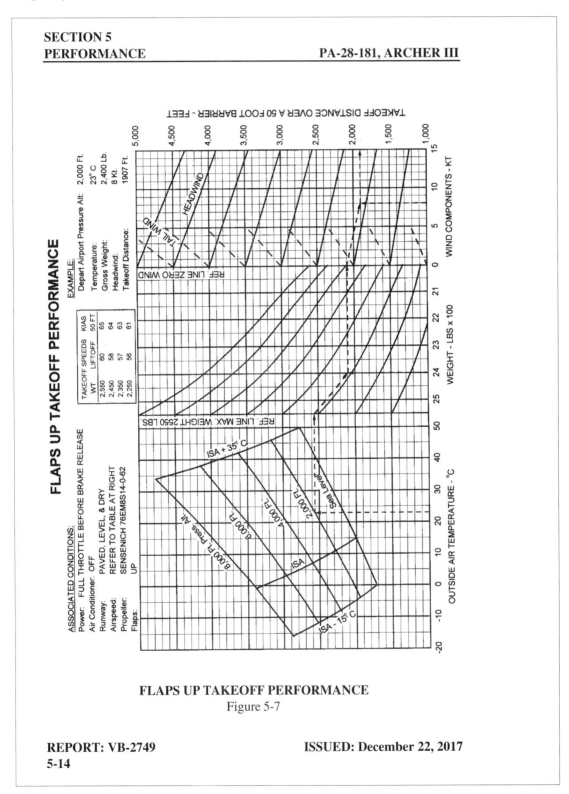

FLAPS UP TAKEOFF PERFORMANCE
Figure 5-7

Flaps 25 Degrees Takeoff Performance Chart

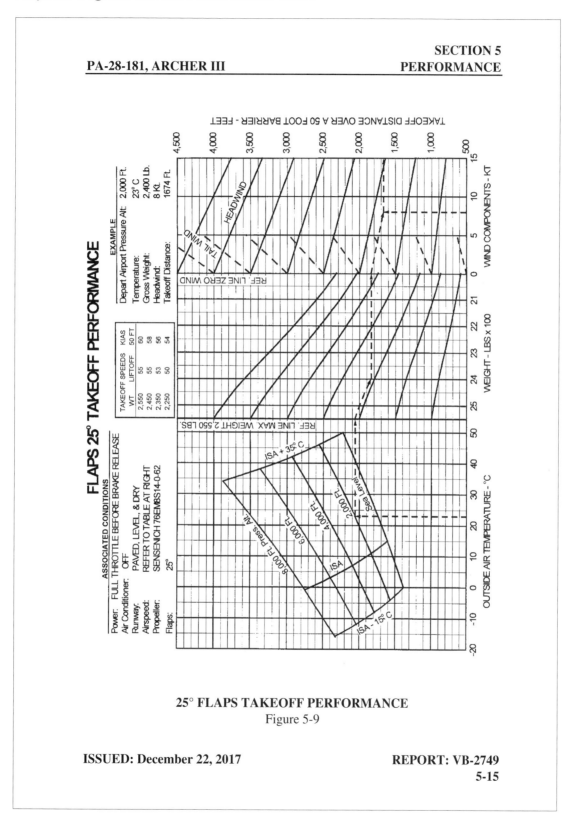

SECTION 5
PERFORMANCE

PA-28-181, ARCHER III

FLAPS 25° TAKEOFF PERFORMANCE

ASSOCIATED CONDITIONS

Power: FULL THROTTLE BEFORE BRAKE RELEASE
Air Conditioner: OFF
Runway: PAVED, LEVEL & DRY
Airspeed: REFER TO TABLE AT RIGHT
Propeller: SENSENICH 76EM8S14-0-62
Flaps: 25°

EXAMPLE

Depart Airport Pressure Alt: 2,000 Ft.
Temperature: 23° C
Gross Weight: 2,400 Lb.
Headwind: 8 Kt.
Takeoff Distance: 1674 Ft.

TAKEOFF SPEEDS		KIAS
WT	LIFTOFF	50 FT
2,550	55	60
2,450	55	58
2,350	53	56
2,250	50	54

25° FLAPS TAKEOFF PERFORMANCE
Figure 5-9

ISSUED: December 22, 2017

REPORT: VB-2749
5-15

Flaps Up Takeoff Ground Roll Chart

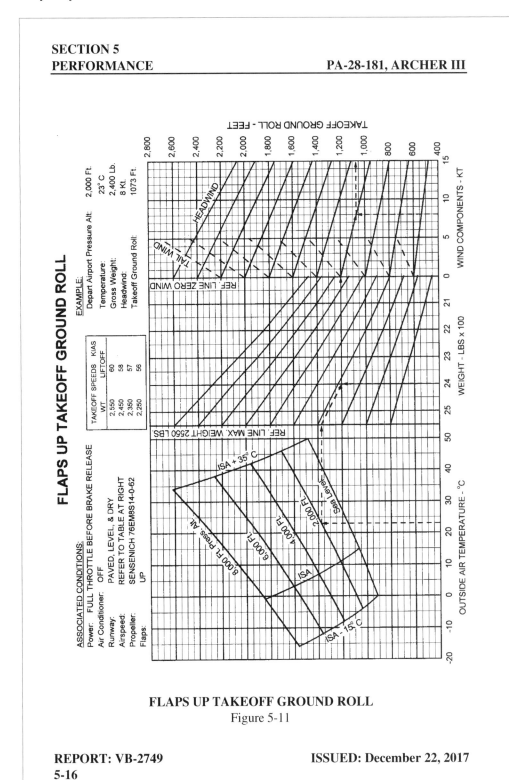

SECTION 5
PERFORMANCE   PA-28-181, ARCHER III

FLAPS UP TAKEOFF GROUND ROLL

EXAMPLE:

Depart Airport Pressure Alt:	2,000 Ft.
Temperature:	23° C
Gross Weight:	2,400 Lb.
Headwind:	8 Kt.
Takeoff Ground Roll:	1073 Ft.

ASSOCIATED CONDITIONS:

Power:	FULL THROTTLE BEFORE BRAKE RELEASE
Air Conditioner:	OFF
Runway:	PAVED, LEVEL, & DRY
Airspeed:	REFER TO TABLE AT RIGHT
Propeller:	SENSENICH 76EM8S14-0-62
Flaps:	UP

TAKEOFF SPEEDS KIAS		
WT	LIFTOFF	
2,550	60	
2,450	58	
2,350	57	
2,250	56	

FLAPS UP TAKEOFF GROUND ROLL
Figure 5-11

REPORT: VB-2749   ISSUED: December 22, 2017
5-16

Flaps 25 Degrees Takeoff Ground Roll Chart

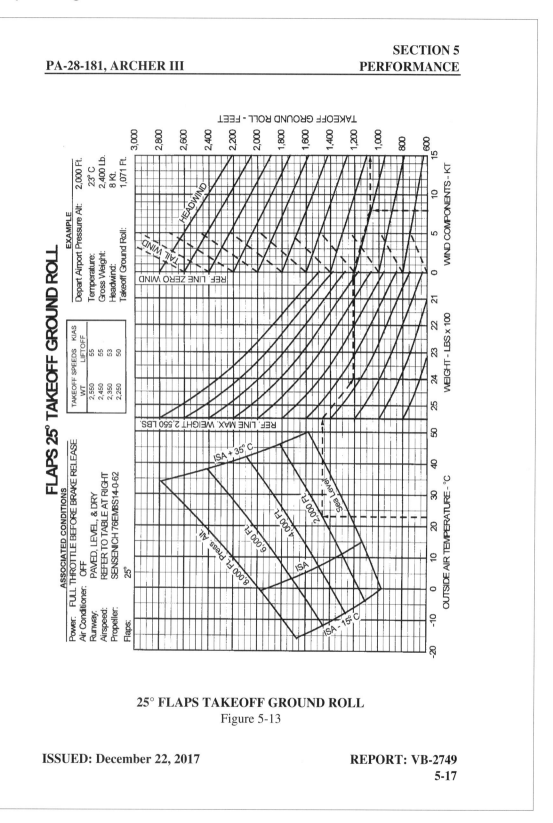

25° FLAPS TAKEOFF GROUND ROLL
Figure 5-13

ISSUED: December 22, 2017

REPORT: VB-2749
5-17

ACTIVITY 3: Landing Charts

(The following charts are from the Piper Archer III PA-28-181 POH. For example only; do not use for flight planning.)

Landing Performance Chart

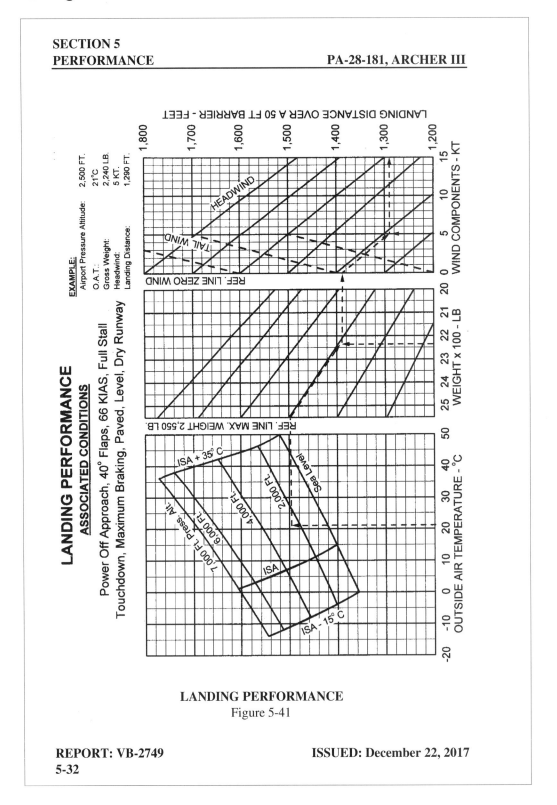

SECTION 5
PERFORMANCE   PA-28-181, ARCHER III

EXAMPLE:
Airport Pressure Altitude: 2,500 FT.
O.A.T.:   21°C
Gross Weight: 2,240 LB.
Headwind: 5 KT.
Landing Distance: 1,290 FT.

LANDING PERFORMANCE
ASSOCIATED CONDITIONS
Power Off Approach, 40° Flaps, 66 KIAS, Full Stall
Touchdown, Maximum Braking, Paved, Level, Dry Runway

LANDING PERFORMANCE
Figure 5-41

REPORT: VB-2749   ISSUED: December 22, 2017
5-32

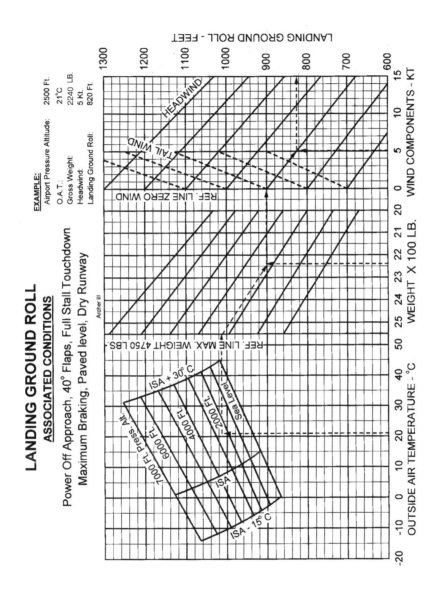

LANDING GROUND ROLL
Figure 5-43

ISSUED: December 22, 2017

REPORT: VB-2749
5-33

ACTIVITY 4: Performance Worksheet

1. Determine the pressure altitude for the following altimeter settings. Use the Grand Forks, ND, field elevation of 845 feet.

   a. Altimeter setting: 29.95

      Pressure altitude: _____

   b. Altimeter setting: 30.12

      Pressure altitude: _____

   c. Altimeter setting: 29.84

      Pressure altitude: _____

2. What is the takeoff ground roll distance (flaps up) with an aircraft weight of 2,500 pounds and the following weather?

   a. Pressure altitude is 3,000 feet and temperature is 30°C.

      _____

   b. Pressure altitude is 1,000 feet and temperature is 10°C.

      _____

   c. Pressure altitude is 1,500 feet and temperature is 10°C.

      _____

   d. Pressure altitude is 2,000 feet and temperature is 25°C.

      _____

3. What is the takeoff distance (flaps up) over a 50-foot barrier with an aircraft weight of 2,450 pounds and the following weather?

   a. Pressure altitude is 1,000 feet and temperature is 0°C.

      _____

   b. Pressure altitude is 1,500 feet and temperature is 10°C.

      _____

   c. Pressure altitude is 2,000 feet and temperature is 15°C.

      _____

4. What is the takeoff ground roll distance (flaps 25 degrees) with an aircraft weight of 2,350 pounds and the following weather?

   a. Pressure altitude is 1,000 feet, temperature is 15°C, and there is a 9-knot headwind.

      _____

   b. Pressure altitude is 2,500 feet, temperature is 25°C, and there is a 2-knot tailwind.

      _____

c. Pressure altitude is 2,000 feet, temperature is 5°C, and there is a 5-knot tailwind.

_____

5. What is the landing ground roll distance with an aircraft weight of 2,400 pounds and the following weather?
   a. Pressure altitude is 3,000 feet and temperature is 5°C.

   _____

   b. Pressure altitude is 1,000 feet and temperature is 20°C.

   _____

   c. Pressure altitude is 1,500 feet and temperature is 15°C.

   _____

   d. Pressure altitude is 2,000 feet and temperature is 30°C.

   _____

6. What is the landing distance over a 50-foot barrier with an aircraft weight of 2,350 pounds and the following weather?
   a. Pressure altitude is 1,000 feet and temperature is 0°C.

   _____

   b. Pressure altitude is 1,500 feet and temperature is 10°C.

   _____

   c. Pressure altitude is 2,000 feet and temperature is 15°C.

   _____

7. What is the landing ground roll distance with an aircraft weight of 2,500 pounds and the following weather?
   a. Pressure altitude is 1,000 feet, temperature is 15°C, and there is a 9-knot headwind.

   _____

   b. Pressure altitude is 2,500 feet, temperature is 25°C, and there is a 2-knot tailwind.

   _____

   c. Pressure altitude is 2,000 feet and temperature is 5°C.

   _____

   d. Pressure altitude is 1,500 feet and temperature is 10°C.

   _____

LESSON 5

ENROUTE, CLIMB, AND DESCENT PERFORMANCE CHARTS

ACTIVITY 1: Aspen, Colorado, Airport

Picture of Aspen, Colorado, Airport

▶ Aspen-Pitkin Airport (KASE).[1]

What do you notice about this picture in regard to factors that affect the performance of an aircraft?

_____

_____

_____

_____

_____

---

1   Photo by Avitya (https://commons.wikimedia.org/wiki/File:KASE_RWY33.jpg), public domain.

Airport Information for Aspen-Pitkin County Airport (KASE)

ASPEN—PITKIN CO/SARDY FLD (ASE)(KASE) 3 NW UTC–7(–6DT) N39º13.31´ W106º52.09´ **DENVER**

7838   B   TPA—See Remarks   Class I, ARFF Index B   NOTAM FILE ASE   **H–3E, L–9E**

RWY 15–33: H8006X100 (ASPH–GRVD) S–80, D–100, 2D–160   **IAP, AD**

   PCN 28 F/B/X/U   MIRL

   RWY 15: MALSF. PAPI(P4L)—GA 3.5º TCH 56´. 1.9% up.

   RWY 33: REIL. Thld dsplcd 1000´. Road. Rgt tfc. 2.0% down.

RUNWAY DECLARED DISTANCE INFORMATION

   RWY 15: TORA–7006   TODA–7006   ASDA–7006   LDA–7006

   RWY 33: TORA–8006   TODA–8006   ASDA–8006   LDA–8006

SERVICE: S2 **FUEL** 100LL, JET A1+   **OX** 1, 3   **LGT** BCN LGTS OPS
dusk–0600Z‡. When ATCT CLSD ACTVT MALSF RWY 15; REIL RWY
33; PAPI RWY 15; MIRL RWY 15–33—CTAF. RWY 15 PAPI UNUSBL
BYD 4 NM FM RWY THR and BYD 7 DEGS RGT of RWY CNTRLN.

AIRPORT REMARKS: Attended 1400–0600Z‡. Arpt CLOSED
0600–1400Z‡. Birds and other wildlife on and invof rwys. Watch for
wildlife on or near rwys. All arriving acft from 2000 to 2300 local
must announce CTAF 118.85 when they are 20, 15, 10 and 5 miles
out and on short final. Equipment may be on the rwy. For acft svc ctc
UNICOM. Hang gliders, para glider s, hot air balloons and glider ops
on and invof arpt up to 18,000´ MS L. All commercial acft advise prior
to pushback onto Twy A. Arpt lctd in high mountain valley with
mountainous terrain from 12,500´–14,000´ MSL in near proximity

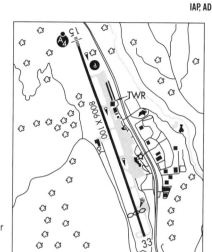

to arpt, numerous unlgtd obst. All adverse wx situations magnified in mountains. Arpt rstd to max acft wingspan of 95´.
Ops dur periods of reduced visibility disc ouraged for pilots unfamiliar with area. Unless ceilings are at least 2000´ abv
highest terrain and visibility is 15 miles or more, mountain flyi ng is not recommended. Due to high apch minimums pilots
may need an IFR alternate even though wx is forecast to be higher than 2000´–3,000´. Terrain will not allow for normal
tfc patterns. High rates of descent may be rqrd due to terrain and lcl procedures. Unique VFR dep procedures exist, call
arpt ops 970–920–5760, or FBO 970–920–2016 for more info. FBO rqr 2 hrs advance ntc for staging acft prior to dep.
NS ABTMT procedures in effect, ctc arpt ops 970–920–5760 ext 0. For all general aviation ops btn 30 min after SS to
0600Z‡ the following applies, acft equipped as rqrd under FA R 91.205(D) for instr flt, pilo t is instrument rated, VFR
pilot–in–command has completed at least one tkf or ldg in the preceding 12 months at ASE. IFR, execute apch/dep
procedures with ATC clnc. Acft rqrg IFR should file flt plan with flt svc 45 min prior to es timated dep. PPR for tkf on Rwy
15 ctc FBO 970–920–2016. Review of airplane performance re commended incl density altitude, weight and balance and
climb performance. Due to poor visibility in valley, use ldg lgts in tfc pat. TPA for light ACFT 9023(1185), TPA for heavy
ACFT 9523(1685). Unctl tfc on the ramps. Rwy 33 run–up area not visible from twr. Pilots are responsible for pax in
ramp area. Pedestrians and vehicles cann ot enter twys without ATC clnc. Stay on the solid side of the red boundary
marking line. Cold temperature rstd arpt. Alt correction required at or blo –26C. Ldg fee. NOTE: See Special
Notices—Special Procedures Aspen County/Sardy Field (KASE) Aspen, Colorado, "Cozy One VFR Departure (KASE)".

(FAA)

ACTIVITY 2: Climb Performance Chart

Climb Performance Chart

(From the Piper Archer III PA-28-181 POH. For example only; do not use for flight planning.)

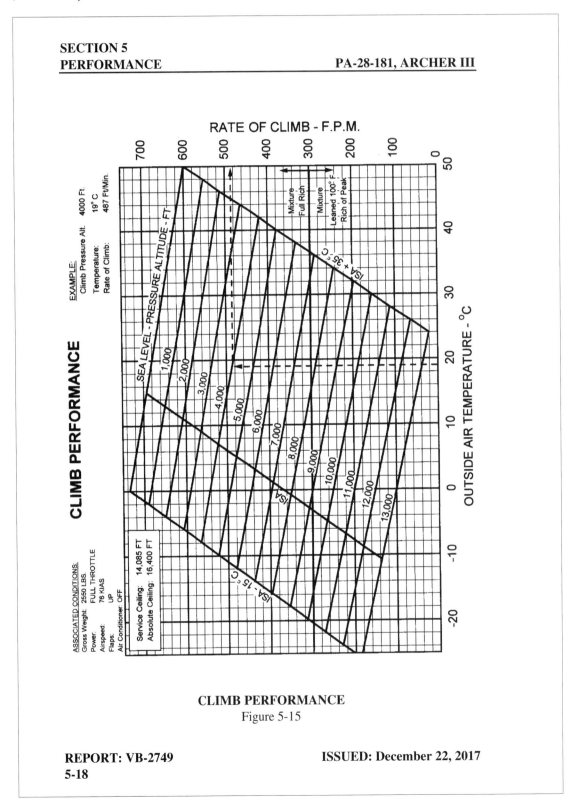

CLIMB PERFORMANCE
Figure 5-15

ACTIVITY 3: Time, Fuel, Distance to Climb

Time, Fuel, Distance to Climb Chart

(From the Piper Archer III PA-28-181 POH. For example only; do not use for flight planning.)

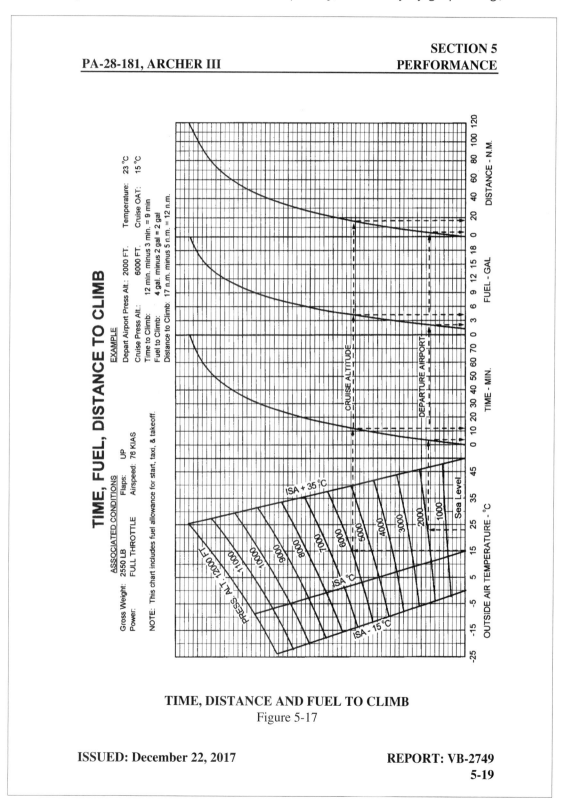

TIME, DISTANCE AND FUEL TO CLIMB
Figure 5-17

ISSUED: December 22, 2017

REPORT: VB-2749
5-19

Time, Fuel, Distance to Climb Example

	Time	Fuel	Distance
Cruise Pressure Altitude			
Departure Pressure Altitude	–	–	–

Time, Fuel, Distance to Climb Practice Problems

For the following questions, assume International Standard Atmospheric (ISA) conditions exist. Refer to the Time, Fuel, Distance to Climb chart for the Piper Archer (PA-28-181) provided on the previous page.

1. Flight information: You are planning to cruise at 3,500 feet. The field elevation is 1,000 feet.

   a. How long will it take you to climb?

   _____

   b. How much fuel will you use in the climb?

   _____

   c. How many miles will it take you to climb?

   _____

2. Flight information: You are planning to cruise at 4,500 feet. The field elevation is 2,000 feet.

   a. How long will it take you to climb?

   _____

   b. How much fuel will you use in the climb?

   _____

   c. How many miles will it take you to climb?

   _____

3. Flight information: You are planning to cruise at 6,500 feet. The field elevation is sea level.

   a. How long will it take you to climb?

   _____

   b. How much fuel will you use in the climb?

   _____

   c. How many miles will it take you to climb?

   _____

ACTIVITY 4: Time, Fuel, Distance to Descend

Time, Fuel, Distance to Descend Chart

(From the Piper Archer III PA-28-181 POH. For example only; do not use for flight planning.)

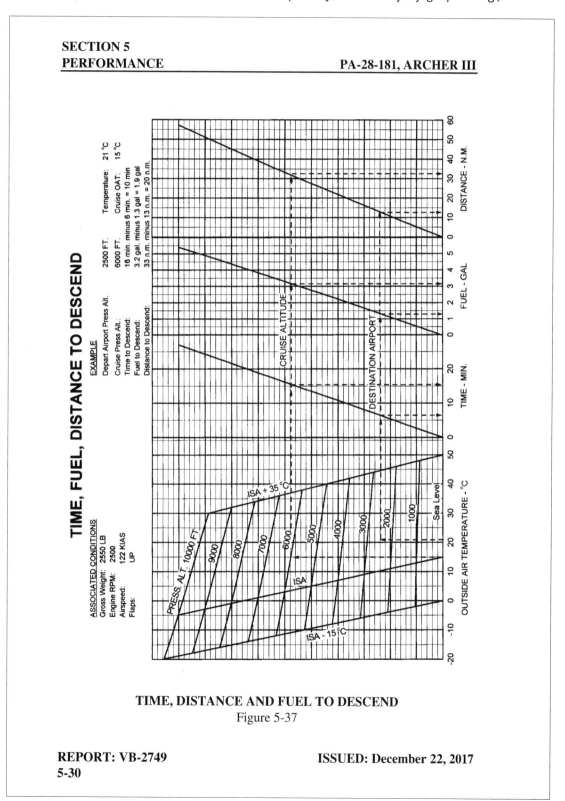

Time, Fuel, Distance to Descend Practice Problems

For the following questions, assume International Standard Atmospheric (ISA) conditions exist. Refer to the Time, Fuel, Distance to Descend chart for the Piper Archer (PA-28-181) provided on the previous page.

1. Flight information: You are planning to cruise at 2,500 feet. The field elevation is 1,000 feet.

    a. How long will it take you to descend?

    _____

    b. How much fuel will you use in the descent?

    _____

    c. How many miles will it take you to descend?

    _____

2. Flight information: You are planning to cruise at 8,500 feet. The field elevation is 2,000 feet.

    a. How long will it take you to descend?

    _____

    b. How much fuel did you use in the descent?

    _____

    c. How many miles will it take you to descend?

    _____

3. Flight information: You are planning to cruise at 5,500 feet. The field elevation is sea level.

    a. How long will it take you to descend?

    _____

    b. How much fuel will you use in the descent?

    _____

    c. How many miles will it take you to descend?

    _____

ACTIVITY 5: Engine/Cruise Performance

(The following charts are from the Piper Archer III PA-28-181 POH. For example only; do not use for flight planning.)

Engine/Cruise Performance (55%) Chart

PA-28-181, ARCHER III

SECTION 5
PERFORMANCE

Engine / Cruise Performance for Non-ISA OAT*
RPM for Constant 55% Power
Fuel Flow: Best Economy Mixture, 8.2 GPH

Pressure Altitude Feet	Indicated Outside Air Temperature			Engine Speed RPM	True Air Speed Knots **
	°C	°C	°F		
Sea Level	ISA-15	0	32	2245	105
	ISA	15	59	2265	
	ISA +10	25	77	2275	
	ISA +20	35	95	2285	
	ISA +30	45	113	2295	106
2000	ISA -15	-4	25	2265	106
	ISA	11	52	2280	
	ISA +10	21	70	2295	
	ISA +20	31	88	2305	
	ISA +30	41	106	2315	107
4000	ISA -15	-8	18	2285	106
	ISA	7	45	2300	
	ISA +10	17	63	2315	
	ISA +20	27	81	2325	
	ISA +30	37	99	2335	108
6000	ISA -15	-12	10	2305	107
	ISA	3	37	2320	
	ISA +10	13	55	2330	
	ISA +20	23	73	2345	
	ISA +30	33	91	2355	108
8000	ISA -15	-16	3	2320	107
	ISA	-1	30	2340	
	ISA +10	9	48	2350	
	ISA +17.5	16.5	62	2360	108
9000	ISA -15	-18	0	2330	107
	ISA	-3	27	2350	
	ISA +8.5	5.5	42	2360	108
10000	ISA - 15	-20	-4	2340	107
	ISA	-5	23	2360	108

NOTE: * Aircraft weight 2550 Lbs., Wheel pants and strut fairings installed
      ** Subtract 3 KTAS if wheel pants are removed.

ENGINE/CRUISE PERFORMANCE (55%)
Figure 5-21

ISSUED: December 22, 2017

REPORT: VB-2749
5-21

Engine/Cruise Performance (65%) Chart

Engine / Cruise Performance for Non-ISA OAT*
RPM for Constant 65% Power
Fuel Flow: Best Economy Mixture, 9.5 GPH

Pressure Altitude Feet	Indicated Outside Air Temperature			Engine Speed RPM	True Air Speed Knots **
	°C	°C	°F		
Sea Level	ISA-15	0	32	2385	113
	ISA	15	59	2405	
	ISA +10	25	77	2415	
	ISA +20	35	95	2430	
	ISA +30	45	113	2440	116
2000	ISA -15	-4	25	2405	114
	ISA	11	52	2425	
	ISA +10	21	70	2440	
	ISA +20	31	88	2450	
	ISA +30	41	106	2465	117
4000	ISA -15	-8	18	2430	115
	ISA	7	45	2450	
	ISA +10	17	63	2460	
	ISA +20	27	81	2475	
	ISA +30	37	99	2485	118
6000	ISA -15	-12	10	2450	116
	ISA	3	37	2470	
	ISA +10	13	55	2485	
	ISA +20	23	73	2495	
	ISA +30	33	91	2510	119
8000	ISA -15	-16	3	2475	117
	ISA	-1	30	2495	
	ISA +10	9	48	2505	
	ISA +17.5	16.5	62	2515	119
9000	ISA -15	-18	0	2485	117
	ISA	-3	27	2505	
	ISA +8.5	5.5	42	2515	119
10000	ISA -15	-20	-4	2495	118
	ISA	-5	23	2515	119

NOTE: * Aircraft weight 2550 Lbs., Wheel pants and strut fairings installed
          ** Subtract 3 KTAS if wheel pants are removed.

ENGINE/CRUISE PERFORMANCE (65%)
Figure 5-23

Engine/Cruise Performance (75%) Chart

SECTION 5
PERFORMANCE

	Engine / Cruise Performance for Non-ISA OAT* RPM for Constant 75% Power Fuel Flow: Best Economy Mixture, 11.0 GPH				

| Pressure Altitude Feet | Indicated Outside Air Temperature | | | Engine Speed | True Air Speed |
	°C	°C	°F	RPM	Knots **
Sea Level	ISA-15	0	32	2485	119
	ISA	15	59	2515	
	ISA +10	25	77	2535	
	ISA +20	35	95	2550	
	ISA +30	45	113	2565	124
2000	ISA -15	-4	25	2520	121
	ISA	11	52	2545	
	ISA +10	21	70	2565	
	ISA +20	31	88	2580	
	ISA +30	41	106	2600	126
3000	ISA -15	-6	21	2535	122
	ISA	9	48	2560	
	ISA +10	19	66	2580	
	ISA +20	29	84	2595	
	ISA +30	39	102	2615	127
4000	ISA -15	-8	18	2550	123
	ISA	7	45	2575	
	ISA +10	17	63	2595	
	ISA +20	27	81	2610	
	ISA +30	37	99	2630	128
5000	ISA -15	-10	14	2565	124
	ISA	5	41	2590	
	ISA +10	15	59	2610	
	ISA +20	25	77	2625	
	ISA +25	30	86	2635	128
6000	ISA -15	-12	10	2580	125
	ISA	3	37	2605	
	ISA +10	13	55	2625	
	ISA +15	18	64	2635	128
7000	ISA -15	-14	6.8	2595	126
	ISA	1	34	2625	
	ISA +7.5	8.5	47	2635	128

NOTE: * Aircraft weight 2550 Lbs., Wheel pants and strut fairings installed
** Subtract 3 KTAS if wheel pants are removed.

ENGINE/CRUISE PERFORMANCE (75%)
Figure 5-25

ISSUED: December 22, 2017

REPORT: VB-2749
5-23

Engine/Cruise Performance Practice Problems

For the following questions, assume International Standard Atmospheric (ISA) conditions exist. Refer to the Engine/Cruise Performance charts for the Piper Archer (PA-28-181) provided on the previous pages.

1. Flight information: You are planning to cruise at 4,000 feet and the temperature is 7 degrees C. You are planning to use 75% power.

    a. What is your engine RPM?

    _____

    b. What is your knots true airspeed (KTAS)?

    _____

    c. What is your gallons per hour (GPH)?

    _____

2. Flight information: You are planning to cruise at 6,000 feet and the temperature is 13 degrees C. You are planning to use 65% power.

    a. What is your engine RPM?

    _____

    b. What is your KTAS?

    _____

    c. What is your GPH?

    _____

3. Flight information: You are planning to cruise at 3,500 feet and the temperature is 18 degrees C. You are planning to use 75% power.

    a. What is your engine RPM?

    _____

    b. What is your KTAS?

    _____

    c. What is your GPH?

    _____

LESSON 6

RANGE, ENDURANCE, AND GLIDE CHARTS

ACTIVITY 1: Range, Endurance, and Glide Range Charts

(The following charts are from the Piper Archer III PA-28-181 POH. For example only; do not use for flight planning.)

Range Chart (No Reserve)

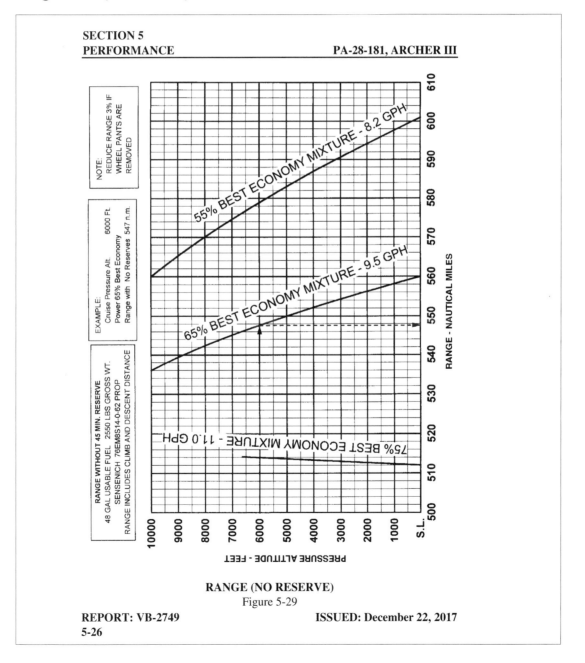

SECTION 5
PERFORMANCE   PA-28-181, ARCHER III

RANGE (NO RESERVE)
Figure 5-29

REPORT: VB-2749   ISSUED: December 22, 2017
5-26

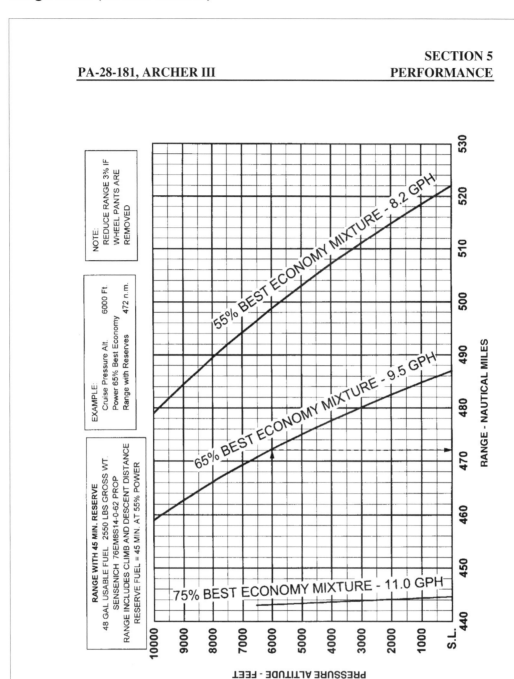

RANGE (45 MIN. RESERVE)
Figure 5-31

ISSUED: December 22, 2017

REPORT: VB-2749
5-27

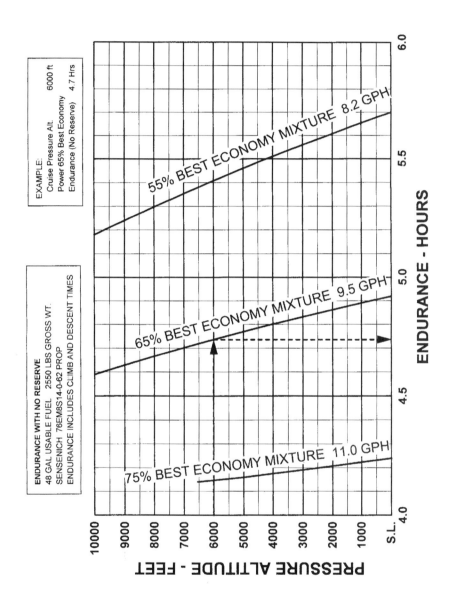

SECTION 5
PERFORMANCE   **PA-28-181, ARCHER III**

EXAMPLE:
Cruise Pressure Alt.   6000 ft
Power 65% Best Economy
Endurance (No Reserve)   4.7 Hrs

ENDURANCE WITH NO RESERVE
48 GAL USABLE FUEL   2550 LBS GROSS WT.
SENSENICH 76EM8S14-0-62 PROP
ENDURANCE INCLUDES CLIMB AND DESCENT TIMES

55% BEST ECONOMY MIXTURE 8.2 GPH

65% BEST ECONOMY MIXTURE 9.5 GPH

75% BEST ECONOMY MIXTURE 11.0 GPH

ENDURANCE - HOURS

PRESSURE ALTITUDE - FEET

ENDURANCE (NO RESERVE)
Figure 5-33

REPORT: VB-2749   **ISSUED: December 22, 2017**
5-28

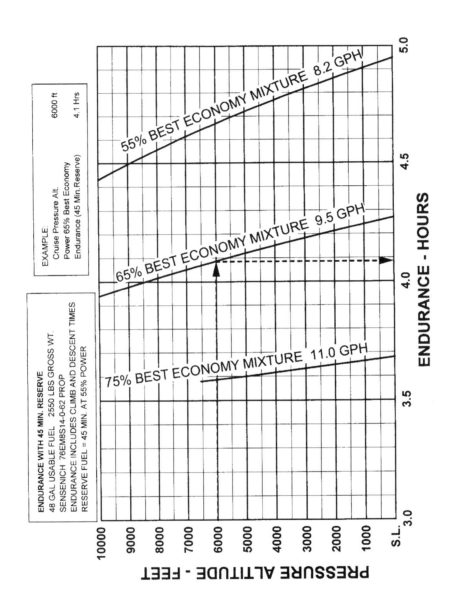

PA-28-181, ARCHER III

**SECTION 5
PERFORMANCE**

ENDURANCE (45 MIN. RESERVE)
Figure 5-35

ISSUED: December 22, 2017

REPORT: VB-2749
5-29

Glide Range Chart

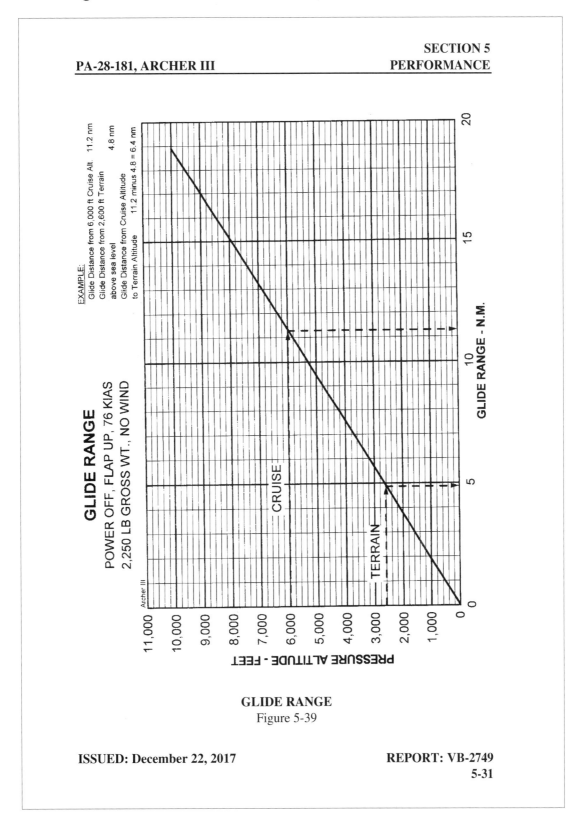

PA-28-181, ARCHER III

SECTION 5
PERFORMANCE

GLIDE RANGE
POWER OFF, FLAP UP, 76 KIAS
2,250 LB GROSS WT., NO WIND

EXAMPLE:
Glide Distance from 6,000 ft Cruise Alt.   11.2 nm
Glide Distance from 2,600 ft Terrain   4.8 nm
above sea level
Glide Distance from Cruise Altitude
to Terrain Altitude   11.2 minus 4.8 = 6.4 nm

CRUISE

TERRAIN

Archer III

PRESSURE ALTITUDE - FEET

GLIDE RANGE - N.M.

GLIDE RANGE
Figure 5-39

ISSUED: December 22, 2017

REPORT: VB-2749
5-31

ACTIVITY 2: Range, Endurance, and Glide Practice Problems

Use the range, endurance, and glide range charts for the Piper Archer provided in the activity on the preceding pages.

Range:

1. What is your aircraft's range if you are flying at 6,000 feet pressure altitude and at 65% power with no reserve?

   _____

2. What is your aircraft's range if you are flying at 3,500 feet pressure altitude and at 75% power with reserve?

   _____

Endurance:

3. What is your aircraft's endurance if you are flying at 5,000 feet pressure altitude at 55% power with no reserve?

   _____

4. What is your aircraft's endurance if you are flying at 8,000 feet pressure altitude at 65% power with a reserve?

   _____

Glide:

5. You are flying at 5,500 feet when your aircraft experiences an engine failure. How far will you glide in nautical miles (NM)? The field elevation in this area is 900 feet.

   _____

6. You are flying at 7,000 feet when your aircraft experiences an engine failure. How far will you glide in NM? The field elevation in this area is 1,500 feet.

   _____

LESSON 7

GUEST SPEAKER: AVIATION PROFESSIONAL

ACTIVITY 1: Two-Column Notes

Name: _____ Date: _____

Guest Speaker: _____ Title: _____

Main idea	Details

Summarize connection to at least one inquiry question:

_____

_____

_____

_____

_____

LESSONS 8 & 9

REVIEW: WEIGHT & BALANCE AND PERFORMANCE

ACTIVITY 1: Exam Review Problems

Directions: Your facilitator will lead you through which of the following questions to review for your upcoming exam on Weight & Balance and Performance.

For these flights, you are flying a Piper Archer (PA-28-181) and should use the weight & balance and performance charts provided throughout this chapter.

Scenario: We are going on a flight today and need to compute the performance planning. Two friends are joining you on this flight. Friend 1 weighs 140 pounds and Friend 2 weighs 190 pounds. You weigh 175 pounds. You also plan to bring your flight bag and another small bag which weigh a combined total of 50 pounds. The aircraft's BEW is 1,658.40 and the moment is 146,518.99.

The current METAR for Grand Forks is:

```
KGFK 311753Z 27009KT 10SM CLR 30/16 A2987
```

Compute the weight and balance for this flight.

	Weight	Arm	Moment
Basic Empty Weight (BEW)			
Pilot			
Front Passenger			
Rear Passengers			
Baggage			
Fuel			
Ramp Weight			
Run-up	−8		−760
Takeoff Weight			

1. Are you within limits? _____

2. What is your takeoff ground roll (flaps up) today? _____

3. What is your landing ground roll today? _____

    _____

You plan to fly at a cruising altitude of 5,500 feet. You are departing Grand Forks International Airport (KGFK).

4. How long will it take you to climb? _____

5. How much fuel will you burn in the climb? _____

6. How many miles will it take you to climb? _____

You plan to fly at a cruising altitude of 5,500 feet. You plan to land back at Grand Forks International Airport (KGFK).

7. How long will it take you to descend? _____

8. How much fuel will you burn in the descent? _____

9. How many miles will it take you to descend? _____

You plan to use 75% power for this flight at 5,500 feet.

10. What is your engine RPM? _____

11. What is your TAS? _____

12. What is your fuel usage in gallons per hour for this flight? _____

13. What would your range be if you were flying at 5,500 feet and at 75% with reserve?

    _____

14. What would your endurance be if you were flying at 5,500 feet at 75% with a reserve?

    _____

You are flying at 5,500 feet and experience an engine failure. The field elevation in this area is 900 feet.

15. How far will you glide in NM? _____

LESSON 10
CHAPTER 4 EXAM

ACTIVITY 1: Current Events Notes

Search for current events relating to communications within the aviation industry. Below, record some of the main topics and issues you discover.

_____
_____
_____
_____
_____
_____
_____
_____
_____
_____
_____
_____
_____
_____
_____
_____
_____
_____
_____
_____
_____
_____
_____

CHAPTER 5

COMMUNICATION

CONTENTS

Check off each activity upon completion.

LESSON 1

AIR TRAFFIC CONTROL HISTORY

ACTIVITY 1: Shocking Facts

In the space below, write down the 1–2 air traffic control statistics that shocked you most.

_____

_____

_____

_____

_____

ACTIVITY 2: ATC History Timeline

Time Period	Main Events
1903–1925	
1926–1935	
1936–1957	
1958–1977	
1978–1993	
1994–2001	
2002–Today	

ACTIVITY 3: ATC History Quiz

1. What was the name of the first air traffic controller?

   a. Leonard Hill

   b. Archie League

   c. Steve Johnson

2. What airport did the first air traffic controller work at?

   a. St. Louis

   b. Chicago

   c. Newark

3. In the early days of ATC, what was used to represent aircraft by moving them around on maps?

   a. Board game pieces

   b. Thumb tacks

   c. Shrimp boats

4. In what decade did the federal government become responsible for ATC?

   a. 1930s

   b. 1940s

   c. 1950s

5. What led to the government realizing that ATC was important and needed to be modernized?

   a. An aircraft midair collision

   b. A strike

   c. Research

6. What is the name of the screen on which controllers reference the radar?

   a. A flat screen

   b. A display unit

   c. A scope

7. In 1980, the air traffic controllers went on strike. Which president ordered them back to work?

   a. Reagan

   b. Bush

   c. Carter

8. Those controllers who did not go back to work were all

   a. given severance packages

   b. fired

   c. told to reapply

9. In 1980, what company developed a computer system for air route traffic control centers?

   a. IBM

   b. Apple

   c. Microsoft

10. At what age are air traffic controllers required to retire?

    a. By their 56th birthday

    b. By their 57th birthday

    c. By their 60th birthday

LESSON 2

EFFECTIVE COMMUNICATION

ACTIVITY 1: Take Home Communication Activity

Part A: Below are the directions that were given in class. To try to improve the communication, write out new, more specific directions for the same picture.

1. Draw a large circle.
2. Draw two triangles on top of the big circle.
3. Draw two smaller circles inside the bigger circle.
4. Color in the inside circles.
5. Draw a triangle inside the big circle.
6. Draw three lines on each side of the top point of the inner triangle.

_____
_____
_____
_____
_____
_____
_____
_____
_____
_____
_____
_____
_____

Part B: Using the new directions you developed in Part A above, read the directions verbatim to a family member or friend. After they have finished drawing, answer the questions below.

Follow up questions:

1. How does their picture compare to the one discussed in class?

_____
_____
_____

2. What did your family member or friend think of the directions?

_____

_____

   a. Did he or she think that anything could have been worded differently?

   _____

   _____

   b. If so, what?

   _____

   _____

   _____

   _____

3. As you read the directions, did you feel that they stated exactly what you wanted drawn?

_____

   a. Explain your answer.

   _____

   _____

   b. Would you reword anything?

   _____

   _____

   _____

   _____

LESSON 3

AIR TRAFFIC CONTROL JOBS

ACTIVITY 1: Air Traffic Control Job Graphic Organizer

Title	
Purpose	
Skills	
Salary	
Airspace they control	
Responsibilities	

ACTIVITY 2: Air Traffic Control Jobs List

Fill out the graphic organizer as you learn about ATC jobs through the presentations and discussions in class.

Job	Airspace they control	Responsibilities
Example: Ground controller	*Ground surfaces of the airport only*	*They control traffic on the ground at a controlled (towered) airport, cleared to taxi and move around on the surface.*

LESSON 4

AIR TRAFFIC CONTROL FIELD TRIP

ACTIVITY 1: News Report Outline

HOW TO WRITE A NEWS REPORT—TEMPLATE
Name: _____
Headline: _____

THE LEAD (Summarize what happened to get the reader's interest)

BACKGROUND (Give background information about the event and more information about the 5 Ws.)

QUOTATIONS (Quote people who were involved in the event.)

CONCLUDING STATEMENT (Conclude with consequences or possible future leads.)

LESSON 5

RADIO TRANSMISSIONS

ACTIVITY 1: Phonetic Alphabet Pre-Test

Directions: Your facilitator will provide directions on how to complete this phonetic alphabet pre-test.

A = _____   H = _____

D = _____   L = _____

I = _____   P = _____

T = _____   V = _____

ACTIVITY 2: Phonetic Alphabet Graphic Organizer

Directions: When your facilitator instructs you to, conduct research to fill out the following table with accurate representations of the phonetic alphabet.

A			N	
B			O	
C			P	
D			Q	
E			R	
F			S	
G			T	
H			U	
I			V	
J			W	
K			X	
L			Y	
M			Z	

ACTIVITY 3: Phonetic Alphabet Post-Test

Directions: Your facilitator will provide directions on how to complete this Phonetic Alphabet Post-Test.

Name (Written using the Phonetic Alphabet): _____

_____

Rewrite this sentence:

TANGO ROMEO INDIA PAPA LIMA ECHO / OSCAR / INDIA SIERRA / TANGO HOTEL ECHO / NOVEMBER UNIFORM MIKE BRAVO ECHO ROMEO / TANGO OSCAR / ROMEO INDIA NOVEMBER GOLF / FOXTROT OSCAR ROMEO / PAPA OSCAR LIMA INDIA CHARLIE ECHO / ALPHA SIERRA SIERRA INDIA SIERRA TANGO ALPHA NOVEMBER CHARLIE ECHO.

_____

_____

_____

_____

_____

_____

_____

_____

LESSON 6

AIR TRAFFIC CONTROL SIMULATION

ACTIVITY 1: Airport Layout Graphic

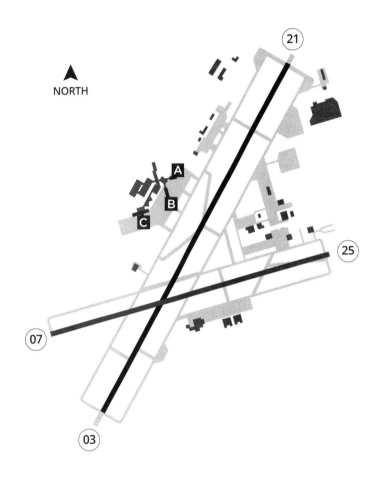

Comments on the runway/airport layout:

_____

_____

_____

_____

_____

_____

_____

_____

LESSON 7

CURRENT EVENTS IN AIR TRAFFIC CONTROL

ACTIVITY 1: Double Entry Chart

Directions: Use the chart below as you read to record and consider the aspects that you find most important or interesting from the current events article. First, on the left side, note a specific line or detail from the text; next, on the right side, tell what you noticed about it, why you chose it, or what questions it raises for you.

Notable Quote or Detail from the Text	Your Observation, Comment, or Question

LESSONS 8, 9 & 10

AIR TRAFFIC MANAGEMENT GROUP RESEARCH PROJECT

ACTIVITY 1: ATM Assignment Description and Criteria

ATM Assignment Description

The facilitator will assign you an ATM research topic. List your topic here:

_____

_____

_____

_____

Research your topic so that you can answer the following questions:

1. Describe your topic.
    a. Include at least 3 things describing it.

2. Why is this important to an air traffic controller or manager?
    a. Include at least 3 points describing why it is important.

3. How does this impact the aviation industry?
    a. Provide at least two examples of how it impacts the industry.

4. Select and answer at least two of the course inquiry questions found below.
   Inquiry Questions:
    1. How does this aviation topic facilitate social, economic, scientific, and/or cultural exchange/change?
    2. What larger concept, issue, or problem underlies this topic in aviation?
    3. What do you notice about how things work in this aviation topic?
    4. What are some things we could not do without understanding this topic in aviation?
    5. If we changed one thing about how this works, what do we think would happen?
    6. How do small changes in aviation affect the larger system?
    7. What is the impact of this part of aviation on society?
    8. How does this part (e.g., ATC, airports, UAS, flight training, etc.) of the aviation industry affect the other parts?

9. What mistakes have been made in aviation? What did we learn from them? What changes were made?

10. What are current issues in aviation? What caused them? What is a viable solution? What would be consequences of the solution?

11. Can you suggest a different way of doing this in aviation?

12. What conclusions about this topic can be made?

13. What patterns can you see across topics in aviation?

14. What reasons might there be for these patterns?

15. How do you think technology might change how we do this in the future?

16. How will automation and/or autonomous operations change how this is accomplished in the future?

Prepare a presentation to explain the ATM topic assigned to your group. You will need to present this material to the class. Each group member will need to talk. Following are the grading criteria.

Grading Criteria for ATM Research Presentation

Student Name: _____

Skill	Points
Spoke during the presentation	____/20
Presentation included:	
• Explanation of the topic	____/20
• How the topic impacts ATC	____/20
• How the topic impacts pilots	____/20
Overall presentation (pictures, flow, duration)	____/20
Total points	____/100

LESSON 11

REVIEW: COMMUNICATION

ACTIVITY 1: Review Notes

Your facilitator will provide directions on how to structure your review notes below.

_____

_____

_____

_____

_____

_____

_____

_____

_____

_____

_____

_____

_____

_____

_____

_____

_____

_____

_____

_____

_____

_____

_____

_____

LESSON 12

CHAPTER 5 EXAM

ACTIVITY 1: Current Events

Article Title:_____

Source: _____   Date published:_____

Write a one-paragraph reflective response to the article that addresses one of the prompts below. Circle the prompt to which you will respond.

Prompts:

- How does this article relate to the key concepts and big ideas we have studied this year, or to big ideas from your other classes?

- What did you learn from the article that you did not previously know? What additional questions do you now have about the topic?

- Identify a problem that needs to be solved within this situation.

- What is your opinion of what you are reading and the issue being discussed? Do you agree/disagree with the writer/creator of this news item? Why or why not?

- How could the knowledge you gained from the event be used in one of the many aviation professions?

- What are some questions you still have regarding this topic?

_____

_____

_____

_____

_____

_____

_____

_____

_____

_____

_____

_____

CURRENT EVENTS RUBRIC

	Exceeds Expectation (4)	Proficient (3)	Partially Proficient (2)	Novice (1)	Non-Performance (0)
Article	Article is well-chosen given topic and inquiry questions from relevant website or news source. All the required information is cited clearly and correctly in MLA format. Article is handed in with the assignment.	Article is from relevant web source and related to aviation. The required citation information is complete. Article is handed in with the assignment.	Article may not be from relevant or appropriate source. The title, source, or one other piece of information may be missing from the citation. Article is handed in with the assignment.	Article may be inappropriate for course topics and important information about the article is missing.	No article submitted.
Summary	Information is clearly summarized and demonstrates understanding of the topic. Includes strong supporting details addressing the who, what, where, when, why, or how questions.	Information from source is summarized and general comprehension is demonstrated. Includes supporting details addressing the who, what, where, when, why, or how questions.	Summary may be unclear, incomplete, copies the article, or is inaccurate. There is a need for more supporting details. Summary is only a few sentences.	Summary is vague, too much information was copied from the article or important details are left out. Details or summary may be confusing.	No summary included.
Response	Student is able to relate article content to class material. Insightfully gives personal response with extremely strong thoughts and ideas. Two thoughtful, inquiry related questions are present.	General connection made between article and class material. Tells what their thoughts of the article are, with detail and description. Attempts to push thinking with some prompts. Two questions are submitted that relate to the field of aviation.	Simple or brief connection made between article and class material. Attempts to tell thoughts about the article. Lacks thoughtful ideas that relate to the article. Only one question present and/or are not applicable.	Attempt made to relate article content to class material. Response is inappropriate to the content of the article. Questions attempted.	No response written.
Conventions	Writer makes little or no errors in grammar or spelling that distract the reader from the content. Paragraphs contain sentences that are well-constructed. There are varied beginnings and rich and appropriate vocabulary.	Writer makes very few errors in grammar or spelling that distract the reader from the content. Most sentences are well-constructed with varied beginnings and vocabulary.	Writer makes some major errors in grammar or spelling. Some sentences may not be well-constructed. Similar words are used too often.	Writer makes many errors in grammar or spelling. Sentences lack structure and appear incomplete or are confusing.	No writing submitted or is illegible.

Suggested grading conversion scale: A = 16-14   B = 13-10   C = 9-8   D = 7-4   F = 3-0

Comments

Total _____ / 16 pts

CHAPTER 6

PEOPLE, EVENTS, AND TRENDS IN AVIATION

CONTENTS

Check off each activity upon completion.

LESSON 1

AVIATION PIONEERS

ACTIVITY 1: Picture Response

Write down your responses to the following statements about the pictures displayed.

I notice _____

_____

_____

_____

So I wonder _____

_____

_____

_____

ACTIVITY 2: Notes Outline

Complete the notes outline during the interactive lecture given by your facilitator.

1. Lighter than air _____

_____

    a. Armen Firman

_____

_____

_____

    b. Abbas ibn Firnas

_____

_____

_____

    c. Leonardo da Vinci

_____

_____

_____

d. Joseph and Jacque Montgolfier

    i. First what? _____

       • How high did it go? _____

    ii. First passengers were: _____

e. Jean-Pierre Blanchard

_____

_____

_____

    i. How high did he go? _____

2. Describe how a balloon flies and climbs in the sky.

_____

_____

    a. How do you land a balloon? _____

_____

    b. Benefits of balloons: _____

_____

    c. Drawbacks of balloons: _____

_____

3. Heavier than air _____

_____

    a. Sir George Cayley _____

_____

_____

       i. Firsts include: _____

_____

    b. Dirigibles _____

_____

    c. Otto Lilienthal _____

_____

_____

ACTIVITY 3: Quick-Think Questions

Quick Think 1: Turn to a partner next to you and complete this statement: "The most similar part of early historical aviation that we still see evident in modern aviation is …"

_____

_____

_____

_____

Quick Think 2: Find a new partner near you. Explain whether you think the following statement is true or false: "Leonardo da Vinci was the first true aviator."

_____

_____

_____

_____

Quick Think 3: How did the Montgolfier brothers apply the engineering design method with their balloon?

- Ask—What problem were they trying to solve?

  _____

  _____

- Imagine—How did they propose to solve the problem?

  _____

  _____

- Plan—What supplies did they need and what steps did they take?

  _____

  _____

- Create—What did they create? (include dimensions)

  _____

  _____

- Improve—What did they learn from their mistakes? How did they improve the design?

  _____

  _____

- Present—How did they present their findings?

  _____

  _____

ACTIVITY 4: Summary Quote Response

How does this quote by Socrates connect to/explain the importance of modern-day aviation?

> "Man must rise above the Earth—to the top of the atmosphere and beyond—for only thus will he fully understand the world in which he lives."[1]

This quote...

_____

_____

_____

_____

_____

_____

_____

_____

_____

_____

_____

_____

_____

_____

1   Dave English, *The Air Up There: More Great Quotations on Flight* (New York: McGraw-Hill, 2003).

LESSON 2

AVIATION HISTORY—WORLD WAR I THROUGH THE GOLDEN AGE

ACTIVITY 1: Introduction Photo Analysis

▶ Capt. Lowell H. Smith and Lt. John P. Richter performing the first aerial refueling on June 27, 1923. The DH-4B biplane remained aloft over the skies of Rockwell Field in San Diego, California, for 37 hours and 15 minutes with the help of refueling from another DH-4. The airfield's logo is visible on the aircraft.[2]

Analyze the photo and record your responses to the following prompts about the picture using the photo analysis process from the U.S. National Archives.

1. Quickly scan the photo. What do you notice first?

   _____

   _____

   _____

2 U.S. Army (https://commons.wikimedia.org/wiki/File:Refueling,_1923.jpg)

2. Type of photo (check all that apply)

Portrait	Landscape	Aerial/Satellite	Action
Architectural	Event	Family	Panoramic
Posed	Candid	Documentary	Selfie

3. Is there a caption? If so, what does the caption say?

_____

_____

_____

_____

4. List the people, objects, and activities you see.

People	Objects	Activities

5. Who took this photo? (Answer as best you can.)

_____

_____

6. Where is it from?

_____

7. What was happening at the time in history this photo was taken?

_____

_____

_____

8. Why was it taken? List evidence from the photo that led you to your conclusion.

_____

_____

_____

9. What did you find out from this photo that you might not learn anywhere else?

_____

_____

_____

ACTIVITY 2: Skeletal Notes Timeline

Identify the key events and people in the timeline below during the interactive lecture given by your facilitator. The years have already been identified for you, and a word bank is provided below the table.

Date	Name or Event	Description or Accomplishment
BC		Made wings of feathers and attached them to his arms with wax. His son flew too close to the sun, the wax melted from the heat of the sun, the feathers fell off, and the son fell out of the sky.
875 AD		Designed a flying machine capable of carrying a human being.
1452		Sketched lots of flying machines including one with a screw link design.
1783		First hot air balloon flight.
1849		Father of aviation. First to think of four aerodynamic forces. Lots of manned glider designs. Used modern engineering terms.
1887		Kite aerial photography by this British meteorologist.
1893		Studied birds. He built lots of gliders and logged more than 2,000 glider flights.
1898		Demonstrated radio control of a small boat to the U.S. Navy.
1900		The prototype LZ1 took flight and carried people for almost 4 miles. He went on to create more successful rigid dirigible airships.
1903		First manned flight in the Wright Flyer.

Date	Name or Event	Description or Accomplishment
1908		Man from the U.S. who championed for the development of aircraft. Created the "June Bug." Flew the first public flight over 5,000 feet, the longest flight to date.
1909		First man to fly across the English Channel.
1914		Development of aircraft, bombers and seaplanes. Lots of engine trouble. Aircraft were used in war for the first time, mostly for manned photographic reconnaissance.
1916		Created Pacific Airplane Company and a year later the company was renamed Boeing Airplane Company.
1916		Recorded his first of many "kills" during aerial combat for Russia.
1917		He began work on an unmanned aircraft, which included the use of a gyroscope to maintain stability. He was labeled the "father of radio guided systems."
1918		The first pilotless aircraft (drone) was developed after World War 1, flying in 1918. It was developed by the U.S. to be used for "aerial torpedoes."
1919		He is referred to as the "Father of the US Air Force." He advocated for the strengthening of air power in the U.S. military.
1924		He was one of the founders of Delta Airlines.
1925		First pilot to complete an outside loop. First to fly completely IFR. Lots of records.
1927		First nonstop flight between New York and Paris.
1928		First woman to fly across the Atlantic. Many records. Disappeared in 1937 in an attempt to fly around the world.
1930		First air traffic controller. Controlled traffic by waving flags.
1932		He went to work for the German army to develop liquid-fuel rockets.
1937		Lots of air races. First woman to enter some of them. Set numerous speed records in various aircraft. First woman to land on an aircraft carrier. First woman to fly faster than the speed of sound. Best female aviator in 1938.

Date	Name or Event	Description or Accomplishment
1940s		Increased the size of the Army and Navy's aircraft presence. Lots of developments to aircraft—P-51 Mustang, P-38 Lightning, Corsair. Better engines, increased weapon-carrying capacity since WWI, increased maneuverability and speed. Jet engines were introduced. Pilot training became very important.
1940s		15,000 drones manufactured by this company for training UAS Army anti-aircraft gunners. The company was owned by Reginald Denny and later purchased by Northrop Corporation in 1952.
1942–1944		Jacki Cochran had a big influence in the creation of this service opportunity for women. They ferried aircraft, provided aircraft training, and provided towing of artillery targets.
1944		10,000 of these drones were launched at London in 1944. It was an early cruise missile used by the Germans.
1947		His work on the "Spruce Goose" was completed. It made its first and only flight that year. This idea led to further development of large transport aircraft designs.
1947		First pilot to fly faster than the speed of sound in the Bell X-1. Was a P-51 pilot, then became a test pilot. Many other records.
1950s		Military pilot who began flying in airshows with both military and civilian aircraft. Very famous airshow performer.
1953		Test pilot who was hired by NACA. First pilot to fly Mach 2, over 1,320 mph. Flew lots of rocket planes, X-15. He logged over 100 flights in these types of aircraft. He was an aerospace engineer who felt that flying was integral to designing the best aircraft.
1961		Test pilot. Was the first man in outer space. From Russia.
1969		First man on the moon.
1969		One of the three Apollo 11 Astronauts. He was the one who stayed in the shuttle.
1970s		Aviation changed the way war was fought. New tactics were developed. Helicopters were used for both reconnaissance and attacks. Jet bombers and fighters were used extensively.
1980s		Aeronautical engineer is credited with designing various UAS platforms (Albatross and Amber) that laid the foundation for today's Predator.

Date	Name or Event	Description or Accomplishment
1982		Use of UAS by Israeli Air Force.
1990s		Lots of missiles and bombs were used. Improved technology and changes in use of aerial tactics. Threat of chemical weapons. Apache helicopter fired the first air shot of the war. Increased knowledge about how aircraft perform in desert conditions—for example, how to care for aircraft/helicopter engines after a sandstorm.
2000s		Military and civilian use. Military uses include collecting surveillance and dropping bombs. Civilian uses include aerial photography, surveillance, and recreation. Sizes range from as small as a hummingbird to as large as a full-size, four-seat GA aircraft.
2000s		This UAS aircraft set endurance record of 33.1 hours in 2008.
2000s		This UAS manufacturer has flown the ScanEagle UAS more than 1,000,000 hours.
2000s		NASA's Mars Rovers. They completed the journey to Mars and have been collecting samples and sending back data and pictures.

Word Bank

WASP, Women Air Service Pilots
Leonardo da Vinci
World War II
Sir George Cayley
Otto Lilienthal
Glenn Curtis
Jackie Cochran
Montgolfier brothers
World War I
Daedalus
Neil Armstrong
Unmanned Aircraft Systems (UAS)
Curiosity and Opportunity
Vietnam War
Abbas ibn Firnas
Chuck Yeager
Wright brothers
Archie League
Nicola Tesla
Bekaa Valley War
Boeing Insitu
Archibald Montgomery Low

Robert Hoover
Scott Crossfield
Louis Blériot
Hewitt-Sperry Automatic Airplane
Jimmy Doolittle
Manfred von Richthofen
Ferdinand von Zeppelin
Wernher von Braun
William "Billy" Mitchell
Gulf Wars
Amelia Earhart
Michael Collins
William Boeing
Howard Hughes
Collett Woolman
Yuri Gagarin
Charles Lindbergh
E.D. Archibald
Abraham Karem
Northrop Grumman Global Hawk
Radioplane Company
V-1 flying bomb (buzz bomb)

ACTIVITY 3: Quick-Think Questions

Quick Think 1: Turn to a partner near you and compare completion of the timeline for accuracy up to this point.

Quick Think 2: Turn to a new partner. Answer the following question together. "The most important lasting implication for aviation from World War I was...." Add your answer to the Backchannel Chat or other online discussion tool specified by your facilitator.

Quick Think 3: Which country's approach to aviation during the time of World War I is most like that of the United States today: Britain, Germany, or France?

ACTIVITY 4: Influential Person/Event Comparison

1. Who or what do you think is the most influential person or event in aviation history so far?

   _____

   _____

2. Explain three reasons why that person or event is the most influential.

   a. _____

   _____

   b. _____

   _____

   c. _____

   _____

3. Compare your answers with a partner. Record below what influential person or event your partner chose and the reasons they listed for why that person/event is the most influential.

   Your partner's chosen influential person or event: _____

   Reasons:

   a. _____

   _____

   b. _____

   _____

   c. _____

   _____

LESSON 3

AVIATION HISTORY—WORLD WAR II, THE COLD WAR, AND THE JET AGE TO TODAY

ACTIVITY 1: Introduction Photo and Video Prompts

Video: Air Traffic Across the World

What's going on in this video?

_____

_____

What do you see that makes you say that?

_____

_____

What evidence supports your observations?

_____

_____

_____

Photo[3]

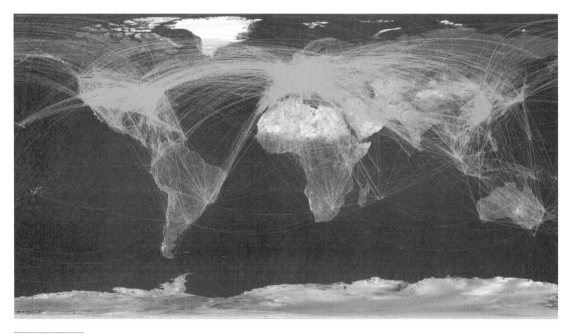

---

3   By Jpatokal (https://commons.wikimedia.org/wiki/File:World-airline-routemap-2009.png), Wikimedia Commons, CC BY-SA 3.0 (https://creativecommons.org/licenses/by-sa/3.0/deed.en).

Use visual thinking strategies and write down your responses to the following statements about the picture:

What's going on in this picture?

_____

_____

What do you see that makes you say that?

_____

_____

What evidence supports your observations?

_____

_____

_____

ACTIVITY 2: Cornell Notes Outline

TOPIC:	
KEY POINTS	**NOTES**
Army Air Forces	
General Aviation	
WWII Aircraft	
Women in WWII	

(continued)

TOPIC:	
KEY POINTS	**NOTES**
Developments	
Rockets	
Deicing	
Navigation	
Pressurization	
The Jet Age	
Vietnam	
Airlines	
Air Traffic Control	

TOPIC:	
KEY POINTS	**NOTES**
UAS	
Regional	
Problems	
Next Gen	

SUMMARY OF MAIN IDEAS

_____

_____

_____

_____

_____

ACTIVITY 3: Quick-Think Questions

Quick Think 1: Do a two-minute writing response to the following prompt: "The most similar part of World War II aviation that we still see evident in modern aviation is …"

_____

_____

_____

_____

_____

_____

Quick Think 2: Turn to a partner next to you. Explain whether you think the following statement is true or false, and why: "The Douglas DC-3 and DC-6 aircraft are significantly different than modern-day airliners."

_____

_____

_____

_____

_____

_____

Quick Think 3: Choose (and circle) which of the following you think is the most important issue to tackle first, based on personal experience/general knowledge:

- Airports
- Air traffic control/management
- Pilot supply
- Free flight or flight paths
- Integrating UAS with manned aircraft into the National Airspace System
- Aviation security

ACTIVITY 4: Summary Activity Prompt

Share with a partner your own thoughts about the photo and video from the beginning of the lesson. How closely do your answers match what is actually occurring?

_____

_____

_____

_____

_____

_____

LESSON 4

FAMOUS PEOPLE IN AVIATION—INTRODUCTION

ACTIVITY 1: Famous People in Aviation List

Review the list of famous people in aviation below. Record the inventions or events that you believe led each person to become famous in aviation history.

Charles A. Lindbergh _____

_____

Wilbur and Orville Wright _____

_____

Wernher von Braun _____

_____

Robert Goddard _____

_____

Nikola Tesla _____

_____

Guglielmo Marconi _____

_____

Archibald Low _____

_____

Elmer Sperry _____

_____

Activity 2: Biography Template

Name	Birthdate (and death date if applicable)

Early Life	Contributions to the Field of Aviation

Later Life	Fun Facts

LESSON 5

FAMOUS PEOPLE IN AVIATION—FAKEBOOK

ACTIVITY 1: FakeBook Template

Use the template below to gather information about your famous person in aviation. Be prepared to share your completed posters with your classmates.

ACTIVITY 2: Venn Diagram

Use the Venn Diagram below to compare and contrast your famous person in aviation to that of your assigned peer. Be prepared to share your results with the whole group.

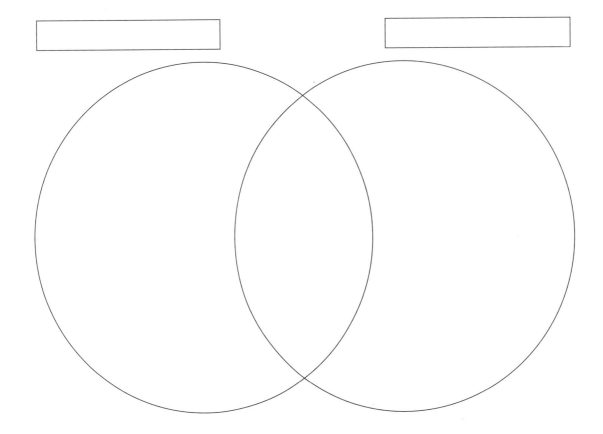

LESSONS 6 & 7

FAMOUS PEOPLE IN AVIATION—RESEARCH PAPER WORKSHOP

ACTIVITY 1: Whip Share Prompts

I notice...

_____

_____

_____

I wonder...

_____

_____

_____

My person is important to the field of aviation because...

_____

_____

_____

I think that....

_____

_____

_____

Because I researched this person, now I know...

_____

_____

_____

ACTIVITY 2: Research Paper Rubric

(See next page.)

RESEARCH PAPER RUBRIC

	Exemplary (4)	Proficient (3)	Basic (2)	Unacceptable (1)
Thesis	Clearly and concisely states the paper's purpose in a single sentence, which is engaging and thought-provoking.	Clearly states the paper's purpose in a single sentence.	States the paper's purpose in a single sentence.	Incomplete and/or unfocused.
Introduction	Strong introduction of topic's key question(s), terms. Clearly delineates subtopics to be reviewed. Specific thesis statement.	Conveys topic and key question(s). Clearly delineates subtopics to be reviewed. General thesis statement.	Conveys topic, but no key question(s). Describes subtopics to be reviewed. General thesis statement.	Does not adequately convey topic. Does not describe subtopics to be reviewed. Lacks adequate thesis statement.
Body x2	All material clearly related to subtopic, main topic. Strong organization and integration of material within subtopics. Strong transitions linking subtopics, and main topic.	All material clearly related to subtopic, main topic, and logically organized within subtopics. Clear, varied transitions linking subtopics and main topic.	Most material clearly related to subtopic, main topic. Material may not be organized within subtopics. Attempts to provide variety of transitions.	Little evidence material is logically organized into topic, subtopics or related to topic. Many transitions are unclear or nonexistent.
Conclusion	Strong review of key conclusions. Strong integration with thesis statement. Insightful discussion of impact of the researched material on topic.	Strong review of key conclusions. Strong integration with thesis statement. Discusses impact of researched material on topic.	Review of key conclusions. Some integration with thesis statement. Discusses impact of researched material on topic.	Does not summarize evidence with respect to thesis statement. Does not discuss the impact of researched material on topic.
Grammar & Mechanics	The paper is free of errors in grammar, spelling, & punctuation.	Grammatical errors or spelling & punctuation errors are rare and do not detract from the paper.	Very few grammatical, spelling, or punctuation errors interfere with reading the paper.	Grammatical errors or spelling & punctuation errors substantially detract from the paper.
MLA Style	No errors in MLA style. Scholarly style. Writing is flowing and easy to follow.	Rare errors in MLA style that do not detract from the paper. Scholarly style. Writing has minimal awkward or unclear passages.	Errors in MLA style are noticeable. Word choice occasionally informal in tone. Writing has a few awkward or unclear passages.	Errors in MLA style detract substantially from the paper. Word choice is informal in tone. Writing is choppy, with many awkward or unclear passages.
References	All references and citations are correctly written and present.	One reference or citation missing or incorrectly written.	Two references or citations missing or incorrectly written.	Reference and citation errors detract significantly from paper.
Deadlines	5 points for rough draft, 5 points for submitting on time, and 50 points for final paper.			
Comments				

Total _____ / 60 pts

ACTIVITY 3: One-Minute Paper

Use the space below to write a summary addressing the following:

"Does your paper have details about the person? Are you making sure you are answering the questions in the assignment description or rubric?"

You will have 60 seconds to record your thoughts below.

_____

_____

_____

_____

_____

_____

_____

_____

_____

_____

_____

_____

_____

LESSON 12

CHAPTER 6 EXAM

ACTIVITY 1: Article Response and Rubric

Write a two-paragraph response that includes a summary and reflection on the following prompts:

"How will robotic pilots impact the number of human pilots?"

"What is your opinion on replacing human co-pilots with robot pilots? Does it matter which is used?"

_____

_____

_____

_____

_____

_____

_____

_____

_____

_____

_____

_____

_____

_____

_____

_____

_____

_____

_____

NON-FICTION WRITING RUBRIC

NON-FICTION WRITING RUBRIC

Category	Exceeds Expectation (4)	Proficient (3)	Partially Proficient (2)	Novice (1)	Non-Performance (0)
Summary	Information is clearly summarized and demonstrates understanding of the topic. Includes strong supporting details addressing the who, what, where, when, why or how questions.	Information from the article is summarized and general comprehension is demonstrated. Includes supporting details addressing the who, what, where, when, why, or how questions.	Summary may be unclear, incomplete, copies the article, or is inaccurate. There is a need for more supporting details. Summary is only a few sentences.	Summary is vague, too much information was copied from the article, or important details are left out. Details or summary may be confusing.	No summary included
Response	Student is able to relate article content to class material. Insightfully gives personal response with strong thoughts and ideas. Included extensive reaction to content, feelings, beliefs, opinions, attitudes and analysis of article.	General connection made between article and class material. Tells what their thoughts of the article are, with detail and description. Attempts to push thinking with some prompts. Included reaction to content including feelings, beliefs, opinions, attitudes.	Simple or brief connection made between article and class material. Attempts to tell thoughts about the article. Lacks thoughtful ideas that relate to the article. Beginning to include reaction to content, feelings, beliefs, opinions.	Attempt made to relate article content to class material. Response is inappropriate to the content of the article. Did not reflect on the main points of the article, did not include feelings, beliefs, opinions, attitudes.	No response written
Conventions	Writer makes little or no errors in grammar or spelling that distract the reader from the content. Paragraphs contain sentences that are well-constructed. There are varied beginnings and rich and appropriate vocabulary.	Writer makes very few errors in grammar or spelling that distract the reader from the content. Most sentences are well-constructed with varied beginnings and vocabulary.	Writer makes some major errors in grammar or spelling. Some sentences may not be well-constructed. Similar words are used too often.	Writer makes many errors in grammar or spelling. Sentences lack structure and appear incomplete or are confusing.	No writing submitted or is illegible.

Suggested grading conversion scale: A = 12–11 B = 10–8 C = 7–6 D = 5–3 F = 2–0

Comments

Total _____ / 12 pts

CHAPTER 7

AVIATION CAREERS

CONTENTS

Check off each activity upon completion.

LESSON 1

CAREER ARTICLE AND INTRODUCTION

ACTIVITY 1: List of Potential Aviation Careers

Use the box below to record the aviation careers your facilitator lists on the board. When the list is complete, circle your top three choices.

ACTIVITY 2: Aviation Career Graphic Organizer

Complete the graphic organizer with the example used by your facilitator. Your facilitator will assign you an aviation career to study in the next lesson.

CAREER EXAMPLE	
Aviation career	
TRAINING	
Location of training	
Cost of training	
Length of training	
Degree or qualifications	
Job duties	
SALARY	
Starting salary	
Salary after probationary period	
Top of salary spectrum	
OTHER INFORMATION	
Potential employer(s)	
Schedules	

LESSON 2

CAREER INVESTIGATION/EDUCATION & TRAINING (DAY 1)

ACTIVITY 1: Aviation Careers

Career Interest Survey Results: Record your top three career interest areas from the survey and two occupations within those categories that you would consider.

Career Area 1: _____

Occupations:

    1. _____

    2. _____

Career Area 2: _____

Occupations:

    1. _____

    2. _____

Career Area 3: _____

Occupations:

    1. _____

    2. _____

ACTIVITY 2: Aviation-Related Job Templates

CAREER 1	
Aviation career	
TRAINING	
Location of training	
Cost of training	
Length of training	
Degree or qualifications	
Job duties	
SALARY	
Starting salary	
Salary after probationary period	
Top of salary spectrum	
OTHER INFORMATION	
Potential employer(s)	
Schedules	

CAREER 2	
Aviation career	
TRAINING	
Location of training	
Cost of training	
Length of training	
Degree or qualifications	
Job duties	
SALARY	
Starting salary	
Salary after probationary period	
Top of salary spectrum	
OTHER INFORMATION	
Potential employer(s)	
Schedules	

ACTIVITY 3: Grading Checklist for Graphic Organizer Responses

GRADING CHECKLIST FOR GRAPHIC ORGANIZER RESPONSES		
Name: _____	Job: _____	
Type of education required		___/5
Where to receive education		___/5
Time required for education		___/5
Job duties		___/5
Potential employer		___/5
Starting salary		___/5
Ending salary		___/5
Total points		___/35

ACTIVITY 4: Concept Map

Write "Aviation-related Jobs" as the main topic in the middle of the concept map below. As your peers present information about their aviation careers, jot down notes related to each career in an empty concept map circle. Include at least one important fact about the career that you found interesting. Add circles as necessary.

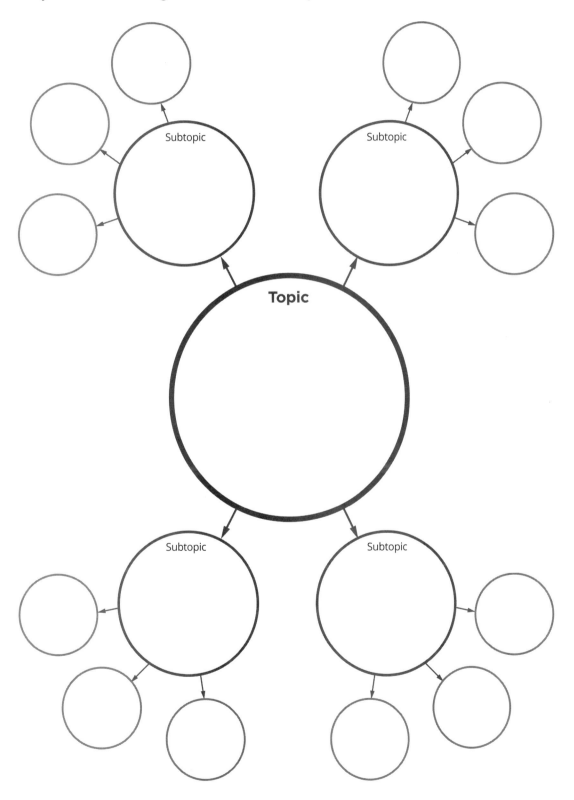

ACTIVITY 5: Concluding Activity:

Think back to the results of the career interest survey from the beginning of this lesson. What aviation career most closely aligns with your current interests and skills?

_____

a. What are subjects in school you should pursue now to have a particular career in aviation?

_____

_____

_____

b. What are some clubs/organizations or activities you could pursue now to become involved in the field of aviation?

_____

_____

_____

_____

_____

c. What are some questions that you would like to ask someone who is working in that career? Do you know someone who is currently working in that career?

_____

_____

_____

_____

_____

_____

_____

_____

_____

_____

_____

_____

_____

_____

LESSON 3

CAREER INVESTIGATION/EDUCATION & TRAINING (DAY 2)

ACTIVITY 1: Personal Characteristics

List personal characteristics that may affect your future career choice in aviation. Record your ideas independently around the outline of the person below. Your instructor will facilitate further discussion.

ACTIVITY 2: Interview Q and A

In small groups assigned by your instructor, create a list of interview questions that you would use to interview an individual in the field of aviation. Record these questions in the left column titled "Interview Questions." Then, your instructor will assign you an aviation career to research. From there, you will independently answer the interview questions your group came up with, according to your assigned aviation career. This completed chart will also be used in Lesson 4.

Interview Questions	Interview Answers
1.	
2.	
3.	
4.	
5.	
6.	
7.	
8.	
9.	
10.	

LESSON 4

CAREER INVESTIGATION/EDUCATION & TRAINING (DAY 3)

ACTIVITY 1: Top Three Careers in Aviation

In the table below, record the top three careers in aviation that you are currently considering. Also include a three-sentence summary explaining why you are interested in each particular aviation career. The rubric for how your work will be evaluated is included below.

CAREER CHOICE 1: _____

Why am I interested?

CAREER CHOICE 2: _____

Why am I interested?

CAREER CHOICE 3: _____

Why am I interested?

One thing I learned: _____

_____

One question I still have: _____

_____

Activity 2: Top Three Careers in Aviation Rubric

TOP THREE CAREERS IN AVIATION		
Criteria	Earned Points	Points per Criteria
Are responses in-depth, thorough, and connected to the interview activity?		___/5
Were all boxes of the Top Three Careers in Aviation table filled in?		___/4
Is the writing clear and easy to read?		___/1
Total points		___/10

LESSON 5

CURRENT EVENTS

ACTIVITY 1: Current Events Assignment Description

Name:	Date:

Purpose: As a global citizen and student of aviation, an industry with worldwide impact, it is your responsibility to keep yourself up to date on global developments. It is also important to see the current industry of aviation as an ever-evolving product of past events, people, and ideas. Gathering reliable information about the world around us and understanding our role, and the role of aviation, in this increasingly connected world is vital. Global citizens should also be able to read closely to determine what a text says explicitly and to make logical inferences from it as well as cite specific textual evidence when writing or speaking to support conclusions drawn from the text.

Part 1: Article

- Choose an article of approximately 250 words in length from a major news magazine, newspaper, or radio/TV segment.

- The article/segment must have been published within the past three months and should address a course topic:

People, events, and trends	Careers
Aircraft (manned or unmanned)	Flight instruments
Airport operations	Airspace
Aerodynamics of flight	Flight planning
Weather	Flight maneuvers
Training requirements	Flight systems
Communication	Flight physiology and human factors

- The article/segment must be printed and stapled to your current event report and turned in with the assignment *or* submitted on the class website as a file or a link to the article.

- Your news article *cannot* be about sports or celebrities! It *cannot* be a blog or opinion-based article. It *cannot* be a local news story!

- Carefully conduct a deep reading of the article and annotate using text markings.

Part 2: Written Response

- Paragraph 1: Summarize the main point(s) of the article in your own words. This summary should clearly demonstrate understanding of the material.

- Paragraph 2: Write a reflective response to the article that addresses at least one of the course inquiry questions. A few prompts for reflective writing can also guide your response.

  › How does this article relate to the key concepts and big ideas we have studied this year or to big ideas from your other classes?

  › What did you learn from the article that you did not previously know?

  › What additional questions do you now have about the topic?

  › Identify a problem that needs to be solved within this situation.

  › What is your opinion of what you are reading and the issue being discussed? Do you agree/disagree with the writer/creator of this news item? Why or why not?

  › How could the knowledge you gained from the event be used in a future career related to aviation?

  › What are some questions you still have regarding this topic?

- Discussion Questions: Write two questions that address the inquiry questions about the issues or events mentioned in the article. These will be used for class discussion.

Article Title:_____

Source: _____ Date published:_____

Paragraph 1: Summarize the main point(s) of the article.

_____

_____

_____

_____

_____

_____

_____

_____

_____

_____

_____

_____

Paragraph 2: Write a reflective response to the article that addresses at least one of the course inquiry questions.

_____

_____

_____

_____

_____

_____

_____

_____

Discussion Questions: Write two questions you still have about the issues or events mentioned in the article that are related to the inquiry questions.

_____

_____

_____

_____

_____

_____

_____

Part 3: Summary

Choose the most important point you learned in relation to aviation careers through the discussion. The group will develop a "headline" statement that captures the essence of the most important point. The group presenter will share the headline with the class.

_____

_____

ACTIVITY 2: Current Events Rubric

(See next page.)

CURRENT EVENTS RUBRIC

	Exceeds Expectation (4)	Proficient (3)	Partially Proficient (2)	Novice (1)	Non-Performance (0)
Article	Article is well-chosen given topic and inquiry questions from relevant website or news source. All the required information is cited clearly and correctly in MLA format. Article is handed in with the assignment.	Article is from relevant web source and related to aviation. The required citation information is complete. Article is handed in with the assignment.	Article may not be from relevant or appropriate source. The title, source, or one other piece of information may be missing from the citation. Article is handed in with the assignment.	Article may be inappropriate for course topics and important information about the article is missing.	No article submitted.
Summary	Information is clearly summarized and demonstrates understanding of the topic. Includes strong supporting details addressing the who, what, where, when, why or how questions.	Information from source is summarized and general comprehension is demonstrated. Includes supporting details addressing the who, what, where, when, why, or how questions.	Summary may be unclear, incomplete, copies the article, or is inaccurate. There is a need for more supporting details. Summary is only a few sentences.	Summary is vague, too much information was copied from the article or important details are left out. Details or summary may be confusing.	No summary included.
Response	Student is able to relate article content to class material. Insightfully gives personal response with extremely strong thoughts and ideas. Two thoughtful, inquiry related questions are present.	General connection made between article and class material. Tells what their thoughts of the article are, with detail and description. Attempts to push thinking with some prompts. Two questions are submitted that relate to the field of aviation.	Simple or brief connection made between article and class material. Attempts to tell thoughts about the article. Lacks thoughtful ideas that relate to the article. Only one question present and/or are not applicable.	Attempt made to relate article content to class material. Response is inappropriate to the content of the article. Questions attempted.	No response written.
Conventions	Writer makes little or no errors in grammar or spelling that distract the reader from the content. Paragraphs contain sentences that are well-constructed. There are varied beginnings and rich and appropriate vocabulary.	Writer makes very few errors in grammar or spelling that distract the reader from the content. Most sentences are well-constructed with varied beginnings and vocabulary.	Writer makes some major errors in grammar or spelling. Some sentences may not be well-constructed. Similar words are used too often.	Writer makes many errors in grammar or spelling. Sentences lack structure and appear incomplete or are confusing.	No writing submitted or is illegible.

Suggested grading conversion scale: A = 16–14   B = 13–10   C = 9–8   D = 7–4   F = 3–0

Comments

Total

_____ / 16 pts

LESSON 6

UNIVERSITY, COMMUNITY COLLEGE, AND TRAINING OPTIONS

ACTIVITY 1: Training Options Worksheet

Directions: Research 5 aviation-related colleges/universities via their official websites. Complete the required information to help you reach your aviation career goals.

COLLEGE/UNIVERSITY 1	
Name of University	
Location	
Yearly tuition	

Aviation Degree Programs Offered (i.e., Flight aircraft, unmanned aircraft systems, air traffic control, airport management, flight education, aviation safety, aviation business, maintenance)

Additional Related Costs (flight, program, and course fees)

Other Considerations (back-up plans, sports, other areas of interest, job placement, internships, reputation, scholarships, etc.)

COLLEGE/UNIVERSITY 2

Name of University

Location

Yearly tuition

Aviation Degree Programs Offered (i.e., Flight aircraft, unmanned aircraft systems, air traffic control, airport management, flight education, aviation safety, aviation business, maintenance)

Additional Related Costs (flight, program, and course fees)

Other Considerations (back-up plans, sports, other areas of interest, job placement, internships, reputation, scholarships, etc.)

COLLEGE/UNIVERSITY 3

Name of University

Location

Yearly tuition

Aviation Degree Programs Offered (i.e., Flight aircraft, unmanned aircraft systems, air traffic control, airport management, flight education, aviation safety, aviation business, maintenance)

Additional Related Costs (flight, program, and course fees)

Other Considerations (back-up plans, sports, other areas of interest, job placement, internships, reputation, scholarships, etc.)

COLLEGE/UNIVERSITY 4	
Name of University	
Location	
Yearly tuition	

Aviation Degree Programs Offered (i.e., Flight aircraft, unmanned aircraft systems, air traffic control, airport management, flight education, aviation safety, aviation business, maintenance)

Additional Related Costs (flight, program, and course fees)

Other Considerations (back-up plans, sports, other areas of interest, job placement, internships, reputation, scholarships, etc.)

COLLEGE/UNIVERSITY 5	
Name of University	
Location	
Yearly tuition	

Aviation Degree Programs Offered (i.e., Flight aircraft, unmanned aircraft systems, air traffic control, airport management, flight education, aviation safety, aviation business, maintenance)

Additional Related Costs (flight, program, and course fees)

Other Considerations (back-up plans, sports, other areas of interest, job placement, internships, reputation, scholarships, etc.)

ACTIVITY 2: Training Options Matrix

As your classmates share their findings, record information from five aviation-related colleges/universities of interest to you.

	Name of University	Location	Yearly Tuition	Aviation Degree Programs	Add. related costs	Other considerations
5						
4						
3						
2						
1						

ACTIVITY 3: Research Summary

Summarize your research by completing the following statement about which training program you would choose, and why.

I would choose _____ because.....

1. _____

   _____

   _____

2. _____

   _____

   _____

3. _____

   _____

   _____

LESSONS 7 & 8

SCHOLARSHIP APPLICATIONS

ACTIVITY 1: Aviation Scholarship Worksheet

Research three aviation-related scholarships. Read through your scholarships until you have found three that you would consider applying for. Enter the information about the scholarships that you have selected into the chart below:

Instructor Example ▼	Scholarship 1 ▼	Scholarship 2 ▼	Scholarship 3 ▼
Name of Award			
Application Deadline			
Type of Award			
What is the dollar amount of the award?			
How many awards are granted per year?			
Who is sponsoring the award?			
What is their email or mailing address?			

Instructor Example ▼	Scholarship 1 ▼	Scholarship 2 ▼	Scholarship 3 ▼
What are the requirements?			
What other criteria should you take note of?			
What do you need to do in order to apply for this scholarship?			
How much time do you think the application process will take?			
Rank the scholarships in order based on how likely you are to apply for each one.			

ACTIVITY 2: Scholarship Reflection

Reflect on the following questions and write your responses in the space below.

1. What special personal qualities, skills, talents, or abilities do you have?

   _____

   _____

   _____

   _____

2. How can you highlight those qualities when applying for a scholarship?

   _____

   _____

   _____

   _____

LESSON 9

GUEST SPEAKER

ACTIVITY 1: Two-Column Notes Graphic Organizer

Name: _____   Date: _____

Guest Speaker: _____   Title: _____

Main idea	Details

Summarize connection to at least one inquiry question:

_____

_____

_____

_____

_____

CHAPTER 8

AERODYNAMICS OF FLIGHT

CONTENTS

Check off each activity upon completion.

LESSON 1

FORCES OF FLIGHT

ACTIVITY 1: The Four Forces

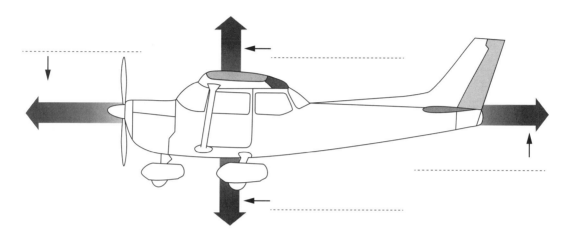

▶ Relationship of forces acting on an aircraft.

ACTIVITY 2: Aerodynamics Graphic Organizer

	What is it? (definition)	Important terms to know	How does it work?	Factors that impact it
Thrust				
Lift				
Drag				
Weight				

ACTIVITY 3: Home Group Questions

In your home group, answer the following questions.

1. What are the four forces that act on an aircraft?

    _____

    _____

2. What are three things that determine the weight of an airplane?

    _____

    _____

3. What are two things that determine the thrust of an airplane?

    _____

    _____

4. A high thrust-to-weight ratio means that the aircraft will have high _____ and a high _____.

5. Write a few sentences summarizing this activity and what you learned from it.

    _____

    _____

    _____

    _____

    _____

    _____

    _____

ACTIVITY 4: Acrostic

Write an acrostic based on one of the four forces: lift, weight, thrust, or drag.

_____

_____

_____

_____

_____

_____

LESSON 2

INTRODUCTION TO AIRFOILS

ACTIVITY 1: Airfoil Definitions

Define the following terms by looking them up in the *Pilot's Handbook of Aeronautical Knowledge* Chapter 5.

Leading edge: _____

_____

Trailing edge: _____

_____

Chord line: _____

_____

Camber: _____

_____

Angle of attack: _____

_____

Relative wind: _____

_____

High-pressure area: _____

_____

Low-pressure area: _____

_____

ACTIVITY 2: Labeling Airfoil Parts

In the drawing below, label the following parts of the airfoil: leading edge, trailing edge, chord line, camber, angle of attack, relative wind, high-pressure area, and low-pressure area.

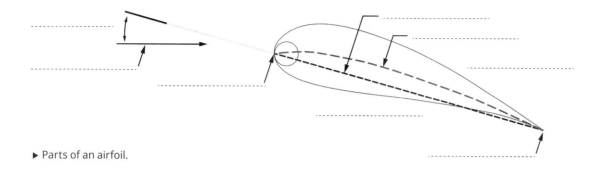

▶ Parts of an airfoil.

ACTIVITY 3: Wing Experiment Questions

Directions: Cut your paper to create two pieces that are each 4 by 5 inches. Keep one piece of paper flat and form a slight arch, loop, or hill on top with the other. Tape the two pieces together.

1. Draw what your wing looks like.

2. How does it react when you blow over the top of the wing?

   _____

   _____

3. How does it react when you blow across the bottom of the wing?

   _____

   _____

4. Why is there a difference?

_____

_____

_____

_____

_____

_____

Create another wing with a different camber.

5. Draw what your wing looks like.

6. How does it react when you blow over the top of the wing?

_____

_____

7. Which wing performed better?

_____

_____

a. Why?

_____

_____

_____

_____

_____

_____

LESSON 3

LIFT—NEWTON AND BERNOULLI

ACTIVITY 1: Label Diagrams

Newton's Third Law

Newton's Third Law states that _____

_____

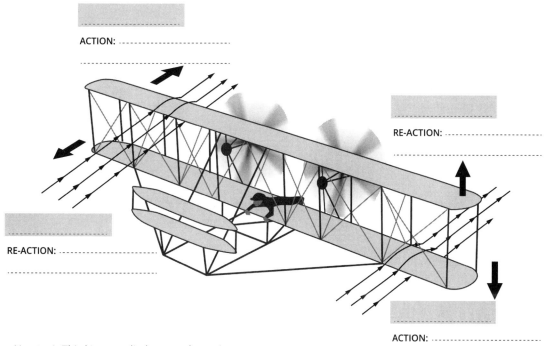

▸ Newton's Third Law applied to aerodynamics.
   (*Adapted from NASA Glenn Research Center*)

Bernoulli's Principle

Bernoulli's Principle states that _____

_____

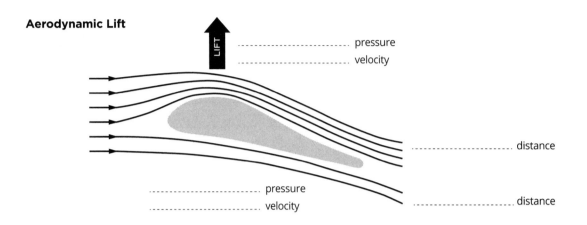

Aerodynamic Lift

▸ Bernoulli's Principle and aerodynamic lift.

ACTIVITY 2: Comprehension Questions Homework

1. Which lift principle relates to the statement "as the airspeed increases the pressure decreases"?

    a. Newton

    b. Bernoulli

2. Which lift principle deals with the airflow striking the bottom of the wing and bouncing off?

    a. Newton

    b. Bernoulli

3. While in a climb, how do you increase the airspeed?

    _____

    _____

4. If you don't touch the throttle, can you climb and fly faster? Why or why not?

    _____

    _____

    _____

    _____

    _____

5. If your payload or weight of the aircraft increases, what happens to your takeoff distance and the required lift for the aircraft? Why?

    _____

    _____

    _____

    _____

6. If you increase the payload, the takeoff speed required is _____.

    a. increased

    b. decreased

    Why?

    _____

    _____

    _____

LESSON 4
DRAG AND DESIGN

ACTIVITY 1: Semi-Truck Comparison

Answer the following questions while referring to the images shown by your instructor.

1. What differences do you notice in the design of these trucks? (Identify at least three.)

_____

_____

_____

_____

_____

2. Why do you think the trucks were designed with those features?

_____

_____

_____

_____

_____

3. What effect would the trucks' designs have on their performance?

_____

_____

_____

_____

_____

4. How do you think truck designers and manufacturers decide which features to include?

_____

_____

_____

_____

_____

ACTIVITY 2: Three-Column Organizer

What do you think causes drag?	How does it work? (Drawing)	How does it work? (Explanation)

Compare and contrast definitions:

_____

_____

_____

_____

_____

_____

ACTIVITY 3: Interactive Lecture Diagram and Notes

Drag curve.

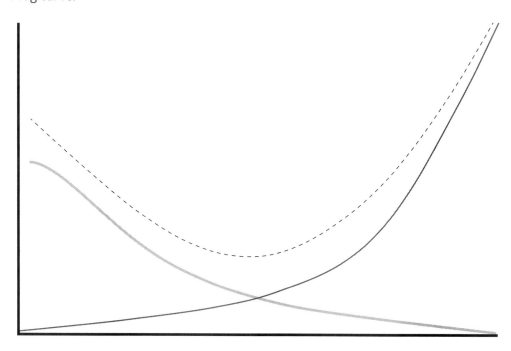

Drag:

1. Parasite drag _____

   _____

   a. Form drag _____

   _____

   b. Interference drag _____

   _____

   c. Skin friction drag _____

   _____

2. Induced drag _____

   _____

3. Lift-to-drag ratio _____

   _____

LESSON 5

STALLS AND SPINS

ACTIVITY 1: Stalls Outline Table

Stalls	Notes from lecture	Added notes from PHAK reading	Added notes from partner comparison
When is a stall likely to occur?			
Indications			
Recovery procedures			
Weight			
CG location			
Angle of bank and load factor			
Flaps			
Power and thrust			
Frost/snow/ice			
Turbulence			

ACTIVITY 2: Spins Outline Table

Spins	Notes from lecture	Added notes from PHAK reading	Added notes from partner comparison
What is a spin?			
Causes			
Phases of a spin			
Spin recovery			

LESSON 6

REVIEW: AERODYNAMICS OF FLIGHT

ACTIVITY 1: Study Guide

1. What is the purpose of wing flaps?

   _____

   _____

   _____

2. What is the purpose of the rudder of an airplane?

   _____

   _____

   _____

3. What are the four forces acting on an airplane in flight?

   _____

   _____

4. When are the four forces that act on an airplane in equilibrium?

   _____

   _____

   _____

5. What is Bernoulli's Principle?

   _____

   _____

   _____

6. What is Newton's law of motion that helps describe lift?

   _____

   _____

   _____

   _____

7. What is the angle of attack?

_____

_____

_____

8. What is the chord line?

_____

_____

9. What is the relative wind?

_____

_____

10. What the term for the angle at which the aircraft stalls?

_____

11. What are the indications that an aircraft is about to stall (this is called onset or imminent stall)?

_____

_____

_____

12. How do you recover from a full stall (either power off or power on)?

_____

_____

13. When you are stalling an aircraft, where on the wing does the stall occur first?
    a. Root of the wing
    b. Wing tip

14. Which power configuration will cause the aircraft to be in a higher pitch attitude in order to stall the aircraft?
    a. Power on
    b. Power off

15. How will frost on an aircraft affect aircraft performance in the following maneuvers?
    a. Takeoff _____

    _____

    _____

b. Cruise flight _____

_____

_____

c. Landing _____

_____

_____

16. Frost is an example of what kind of drag? _____

17. List an example of each of the following types of parasite drag:

d. Interference _____

_____

e. Form _____

_____

f. Skin friction _____

_____

18. What is induced drag?

_____

_____

19. Draw and label induced drag, parasite (form) drag, total drag, and best glide speed on the drag curve.

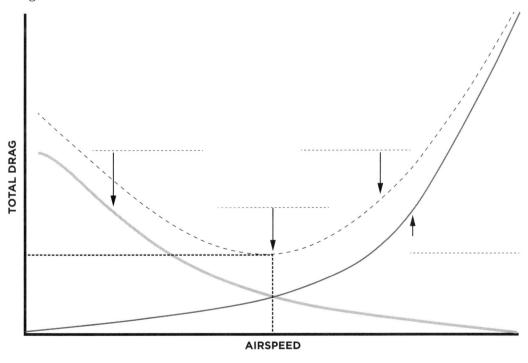

20. If an airplane has been loaded so that the CG is located aft of the aft limit, how would recovery from a stall be impacted?

_____

_____

_____

_____

_____

_____

21. What is torque?

_____

_____

_____

22. What is load factor?

_____

_____

_____

23. What basic flight maneuver increases the load factor on an airplane as compared to straight-and-level flight?

_____

_____

_____

24. If you are coming in to land and are too low, why is it not a good idea to just pull the nose of the aircraft up?

_____

_____

25. Why is it not advised to continually fly with flaps lowered?

_____

_____

26. In general, if you want to fly faster (without increasing the throttle), what should you do with the nose of the aircraft?

_____

_____

_____

27. If you don't touch the throttle, can you climb and/or fly faster? Why or why not?

_____

_____

_____

_____

_____

_____

28. What happens to the performance of the aircraft if you increase the payload?

_____

_____

_____

_____

29. What is a spin and why would it occur?

_____

_____

_____

_____

_____

_____

_____

LESSON 7

CHAPTER 8 EXAM

ACTIVITY 1: Article Response and Rubric

Article Response

Write a one-paragraph response that includes a summary and reflection on the following prompts.

1. Explain the systems and aerodynamic principles the crew worked with to maneuver the plane.

2. Explain which systems failed and how they failed.

3. What mistake was made and what was learned from it? What changes were made in aviation as a result?

Your response will be graded using the rubric on the following page.

_____

_____

_____

_____

_____

_____

_____

_____

_____

_____

_____

_____

_____

_____

_____

_____

_____

_____

RESPONSE RUBRIC

	Exceeds Expectation (4)	Proficient (3)	Partially Proficient (2)	Novice (1)	Non-Performance (0)
Summary	Information is clearly summarized and demonstrates understanding of the topic. Includes strong supporting details addressing the who, what, where, when, why, and how questions.	Information from source is summarized and general comprehension is demonstrated. Includes supporting details addressing the who, what, where, when, why, and how questions.	Summary may be unclear, incomplete, copies the article, or is inaccurate. There is a need for more supporting details. Summary is only a few sentences.	Summary is vague, too much information was copied from the article, or important details are left out. Details or summary may be confusing.	No summary included.
Reflection	Student is able to relate article content to class material. Insightfully gives personal response with extremely strong thoughts and ideas. Two thoughtful, inquiry related questions are present.	General connection made between article and class material. Tells what their thoughts of the article are, with detail and description. Attempts to push thinking with some prompts. Two questions are submitted that relate to the field of aviation.	Simple or brief connection made between article and class material. Attempts to tell thoughts about the article. Lacks thoughtful ideas that relate to the article. Only one question present and/or are not applicable.	Attempt made to relate article content to class material. Response is inappropriate to the content of the article. Questions attempted.	No response written.
Conventions	Writer makes little or no errors in grammar or spelling that distract the reader from the content. Paragraphs contain sentences that are well-constructed. There are varied beginnings and rich and appropriate vocabulary.	Writer makes very few errors in grammar or spelling that distract the reader from the content. Most sentences are well-constructed with varied beginnings and vocabulary.	Writer makes some major errors in grammar or spelling. Some sentences may not be well-constructed. Similar words are used too often.	Writer makes many errors in grammar or spelling. Sentences lack structure and appear incomplete or are confusing.	No writing submitted or is illegible.

Comments

Total

_____ / 12 pts

CHAPTER 9

AIRCRAFT SYSTEMS

CONTENTS

Check off each activity upon completion.

LESSON 1

INTRODUCTION TO AIRCRAFT SYSTEMS

ACTIVITY 1: Skeleton Notes for Aircraft Systems, Part 1

Key Points	Notes

1. Reciprocating engine
  a. Four-stroke cycle
    i. Names of strokes
    ii. What happens in each
  b. Components of reciprocating engine	

2. Propeller
  a. Fixed-pitch
  b. Adjustable-pitch	

Key Points	Notes

3. Ignition system
 	
  a. Magnetos
 	
    i. 5 switch positions:
      • Off
      • Left
      • Right
      • Both
      • Start
    ii. Why have dual
      magnetos?
    iii. P-lead	

4. Exhaust system	

Key Points	Notes

5. Oil systems
  a. Purpose
  b. Oil changes
  c. Oil system emergencies
	_____

6. Induction system
  a. Carburetor
    i. Float type
    ii. Carb ice
  b. Fuel injected
	_____

Key Points	Notes
7. Heating systems	
8. Hydraulic system a. Examples	

9. Anti-ice and deice
   systems
   a. Anti-ice System
      i. Purpose
      ii. Examples
   b. Deice system
      i. Purpose
      ii. Examples	

LESSON 2

ENGINE

ACTIVITY 1: Cylinder Diagram

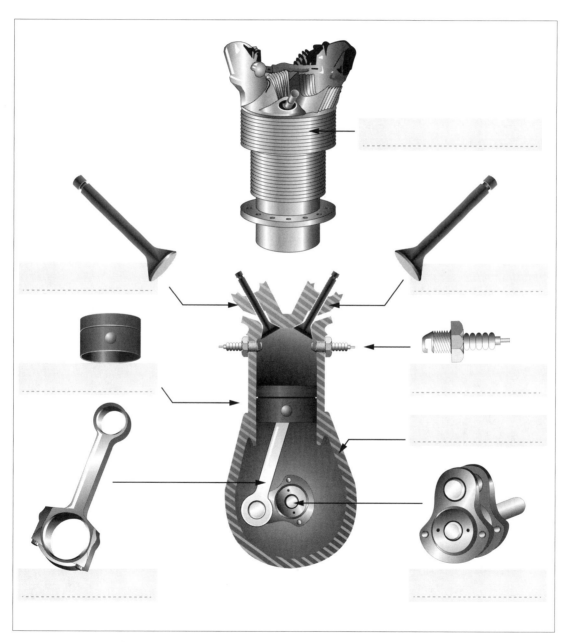

▶ Main components of a spark ignition reciprocating engine. *(Source: FAA-H-8083-25B)*

ACTIVITY 2: Four Square Graphic Organizer

Use the following table to record the name of each stroke and what happens in each stroke of a four-stroke engine. *(Illustrations from FAA-H-8083-25B)*

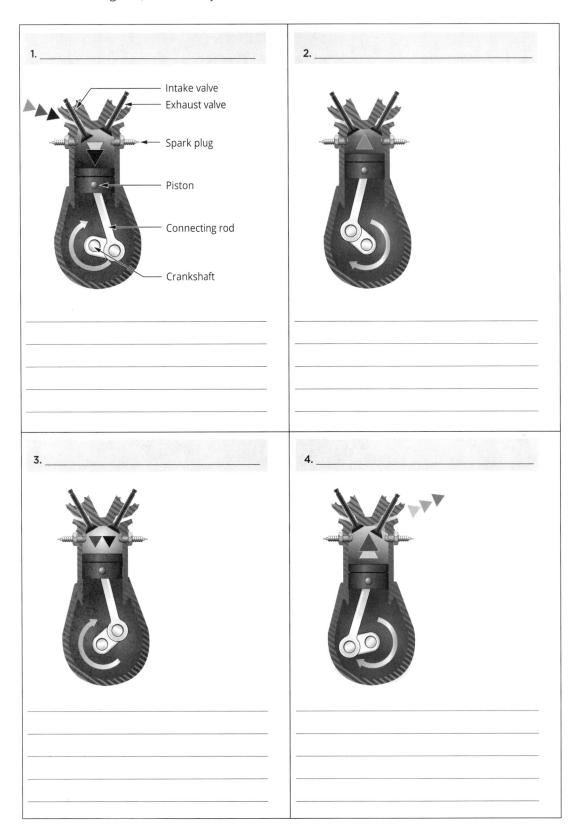

1. _____

- Intake valve
- Exhaust valve
- Spark plug
- Piston
- Connecting rod
- Crankshaft

_____
_____
_____
_____
_____

2. _____

_____
_____
_____
_____
_____

3. _____

_____
_____
_____
_____
_____

4. _____

_____
_____
_____
_____
_____

LESSON 3

FUEL SYSTEMS

ACTIVITY 1: Fuel Systems Diagrams

Label the parts in the following diagrams.

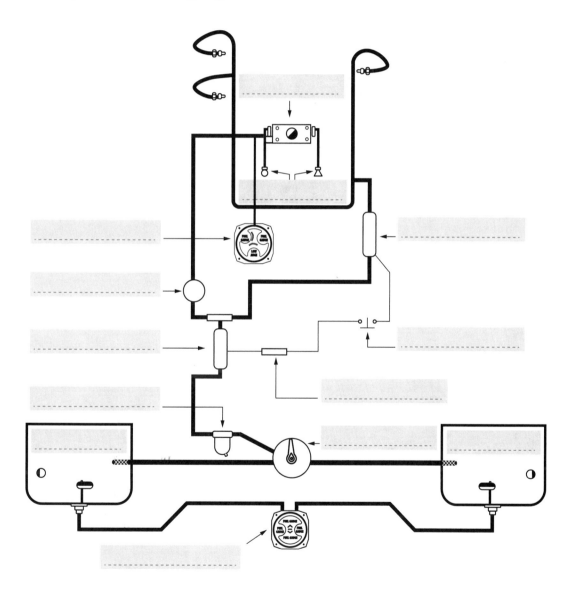

▶ Piper Archer III fuel system diagram from the Pilot's Operating Handbook (POH).
  (Redrawn for clarity from the Piper Archer III PA-28-181 POH. For example only.)

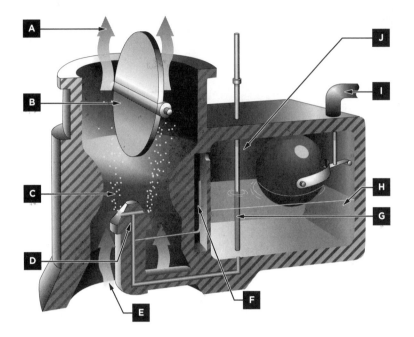

► Float-type carburetor.
(FAA-H-8083-25B)

A _____

_____

_____

B _____

_____

_____

C _____

_____

_____

D _____

_____

_____

E _____

_____

_____

F _____

_____

_____

G _____

_____

_____

H _____

_____

_____

I _____

_____

_____

J _____

_____

_____

ACTIVITY 2: Skeleton Notes for Aircraft Systems, Part 2

Key Points	Notes
1. Fuel systems	
a. Gravity-feed system	
b. Fuel-pump system	
c. Components	
i. Fuel primer	
ii. Fuel gauges	
iii. Fuel selectors	
iv. Strainers, sumps and drains	
d. Fuel	
i. Types	
ii. Colors	
e. Straining	
f. Controls	
i. Mixture control	
g. Leaning	
h. Fuel system emergencies	

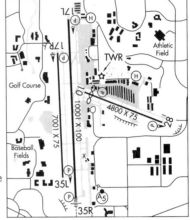

DENVER

CENTENNIAL (APA)(KAPA)   15 SE   UTC–7(–6DT)   N39º34.21′ W104º50.96′
  5885   B   TPA—6885(1000)   NOTAM FILE APA
  RWY 17L–35R: H10000X100 (ASPH–GRVD)   S–56, D–75, 2S–95   MIRL
    RWY 17L: PAPI(P4L)—GA 3.0º TCH 47′. 0.9% up.
    RWY 35R: MALSR. PAPI(P4L)—GA 3.0º TCH 45′. Rgt tfc. 0.9% down.
  RWY 17R–35L: H7001X75 (ASPH–GRVD)   S–30   MIRL   0.9% up S
    RWY 17R: REIL. PAPI(P4L)—GA 3.0º TCH 41′. Rgt tfc.
    RWY 35L: REIL. PAPI(P4R)—GA 3.0º TCH 37′. Fence.
  RWY 10–28: H4800X75 (ASPH–GRVD)   S–12.5   MIRL   0.6% up W
    RWY 10: PAPI(P2L)—GA 3.0º TCH 44′. Thld dsplcd 400′.
    RWY 28: REIL. PAPI(P2L)—GA 3.0º TCH 41′. Pole.
  SERVICE: S4   **FUEL** 100LL, JET A   **OX** 1, 2
  AIRPORT REMARKS: Attended continuously. Self serve 100LL fuel avbl.
  Waterfowl on and in vicinity of arpt. Numerous cranes invof arpt.
  Advisory density altitude displays located at C–1, A–1, and A–18.
  +109′ twr located 1800′ east/northeast of Rwy 17L thld. Numerous
  flood lgts located 1/2 mile north of thld Rwy 17L SS–0700Z‡. Noise
  abatement procedures in effect, ctc noise office 303–790–0598. Rwy
  35R crosswind/base leg north of Lincoln Ave., Rwy 17L crosswind/base
  leg south of Arapahoe Rd. Rwy 17R–35L clsd tfc remain south of
  Arapahoe Rd and east of Interstate 25. Rwy 10–28 avoid noise
  sensitive areas 1 mile east and south of rwy. All acft blo 70,000 lbs
maximum gross tkf weight and Stage lll acft up to certificated 75,000 lbs maximum gross tkf weight may be operated,
one–time exceptions may be authorized by Executive Director on a case–by–case basis. Twy S2 clsd indefly. Helicopter
ops please ctc preferred FBO for ldg zone locations. Helicopter ops on front ramp not advised. U.S. Customs user fee arpt.
Call U.S. Customs 303–768–0309. 24 hr user fee customs avbl. Ctc arpt for fee information. See Special Notices—USAF
306 FTG Flight Training Areas, Vicinity of Colorado Springs and Pueblo Colorado.
  AIRPORT MANAGER: 303-790-0598
  WEATHER DATA SOURCES: ASOS 120.3 (720) 873-2799

> DENVER
> H–3F, 5A, L–10F, A
> IAP, AD

▶ Airport information for Denver Centennial (KAPA) from *Chart Supplement U.S.*

LESSON 4

FLIGHT INSTRUMENTS REVIEW

ACTIVITY 1: Flight Instruments Graphic Organizer

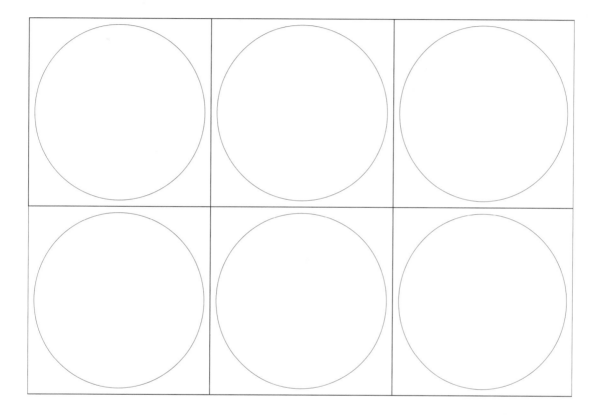

ACTIVITY 2: Pitot-Static Instruments Diagram

Label the components of the pitot-static system.

▶ Pitot-static system and instruments.
(Adapted from FAA-H-8083-25B)

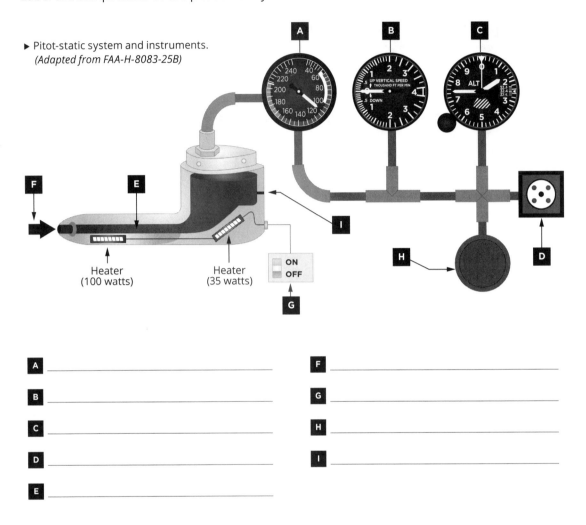

A	_____		**F**	_____
B	_____		**G**	_____
C	_____		**H**	_____
D	_____		**I**	_____
E	_____			

ACTIVITY 3: Gyroscopic Flight Instrument Definitions

Define the following terms during the class discussion or by looking them up in the *Pilot's Handbook of Aeronautical Knowledge*, Chapter 8.

Gyroscope: _____

_____

Rigidity in space: _____

_____

Gyroscopic precession: _____

_____

LESSON 5

VACUUM AND ELECTRICAL SYSTEMS

ACTIVITY 1: Discussion Prompts

1. What is an electrical system?

   _____

   _____

2. What is its purpose?

   _____

   _____

3. Review the pictures of the two cockpits on the next page. What are the differences between the two cockpits?

   _____

   _____

   _____

   _____

   _____

   _____

   _____

   _____

   _____

   _____

   _____

   _____

4. What components in each of these cockpits run off of electrical power?

   _____

   _____

   _____

   _____

▶ Example round dial cockpit.[1]

▶ Example glass cockpit.[2]

1   (Photo by Matti Blume, https://commons.wikimedia.org/wiki/File:Piper_Archer,_Trebbin_(P1090112).jpg, CC BY-SA 4.0,
    https://creativecommons.org/licenses/by-sa/4.0/deed.en)
2   (Photo by H. Michael Miley, https://www.flickr.com/photos/44082489@N00/4850784801, CC BY-SA 2.0,
    https://creativecommons.org/licenses/by-sa/2.0/)

ACTIVITY 2: Electrical Systems Graphic Organizer

Key Term	Important Information	Picture Clue
Alternator		
Generator		
Battery		
Bus bar		
Fuses		
Circuit breakers		
Voltage regulator		
Ammeter		
Loadmeter		

ACTIVITY 3: Glass Cockpit Flight Instruments

Label the flight instruments in the glass cockpit below.

▶ Flight instruments in a glass cockpit. *(FAA-H-8083-25B; FAA-H-8083-15B)*

LESSON 6

REVIEW: AIRCRAFT SYSTEMS

ACTIVITY 1: Preview Questions

Use the following questions to guide your research on the aircraft you selected. Your facilitator may add or eliminate questions as necessary. Be prepared to share your findings.

Aircraft: _____

Fuel System

1. What type of fuel system is it (pump type or gravity fed)?

   _____

2. How many gallons of fuel does the aircraft hold? How many gallons per tank? How much is usable fuel?

   _____

   _____

   _____

3. What type of fuel can the aircraft use? _____

4. How many fuel sumps does this aircraft have? _____

5. Does the aircraft have a primer? _____

6. Does the aircraft have an auxiliary fuel pump? _____

7. Does this aircraft have a carburetor or a fuel injection system? _____

Electrical System

8. Does the aircraft have an alternator or generator? How many volts and amps is it?

   _____

9. Does the aircraft have a battery? How many volt and amps is it?

   _____

10. Does the aircraft have a back-up or standby battery? _____

11. If the alternator stops working in flight, how will you know? What equipment will be impacted? Will the engine stop running?

_____

_____

_____

_____

12. What is an electrical bus?

_____

13. List one item that is on the main bus. _____

14. List one item on the essential/emergency bus. _____

Hydraulic System

15. What on this aircraft is hydraulic?

_____

_____

Control Surfaces

16. Are the primary flight controls controlled by cables and pulleys or are they electrical?

_____

17. Are the flaps controlled by cables and pulleys or are they electrical?

_____

Flight Instruments

18. Does the aircraft have a pitot tube or a pitot static mast? _____

19. Where is the pitot tube or pitot static mast? Why?

_____

_____

20. Where are the static port(s)? _____

21. Is there a vacuum system? If so, what instruments does it power? Is there an auxiliary vacuum pump?

_____

_____

Engine

22. How many cylinders does this engine have? _____

23. Is the engine horizontally opposed? _____

24. How many spark plugs does this aircraft have? _____

25. How much horsepower does the engine have? _____

26. What is the maximum RPM setting? _____

27. What is the maximum airspeed, V_{NE}? _____

28. Is there a prop control in this aircraft? _____

ACTIVITY 2: Research Conclusions Graphic Organizer

Complete the graphic organizer on the following page during the presentations in class.

ACTIVITY 3: Two-Sentence Summary

Record two sentences below that synthesize what all the aircrafts have in common. Be prepared to share.

_____

_____

_____

_____

_____

_____

_____

TYPE OF AIRCRAFT ▶				
How much fuel does it hold?				
Does it have a carburetor or fuel-injection system?				
How many batteries does it have?				
What components are hydraulic?				
Does it have a pitot tube or a pitot static mast?				
Does it have a vacuum system?				
What is the maximum horsepower?				

LESSON 7

CHAPTER 9 EXAM

ACTIVITY 1: Article Response and Rubric

Article Response

Write a one-paragraph response that includes a summary and reflection on the following prompts.

1. Explain why understanding/performing flight maneuvers makes you a safer, professional pilot.

2. Explain how these maneuvers help you understand the performance of your aircraft.

3. Explain how the turn coordinator and attitude indicators look differently in inverted flight.

Your response will be graded using the rubric on the next page.

_____

_____

_____

_____

_____

_____

_____

_____

_____

_____

_____

_____

_____

_____

_____

_____

_____

_____

_____

RESPONSE RUBRIC

	Exceeds Expectation (4)	Proficient (3)	Partially Proficient (2)	Novice (1)	Non-Performance (0)
Summary	Information is clearly summarized and demonstrates understanding of the topic. Includes strong supporting details addressing the who, what, where, when, why, and how questions.	Information from source is summarized and general comprehension is demonstrated. Includes supporting details addressing the who, what, where, when, why, and how questions.	Summary may be unclear, incomplete, copies the article, or is inaccurate. There is a need for more supporting details. Summary is only a few sentences.	Summary is vague, too much information was copied from the article, or important details are left out. Details or summary may be confusing.	No summary included.
Reflection	Student is able to relate article content to class material. Insightfully gives personal response with extremely strong thoughts and ideas. Two thoughtful, inquiry related questions are present.	General connection made between article and class material. Tells what their thoughts of the article are, with detail and description. Attempts to push thinking with some prompts. Two questions are submitted that relate to the field of aviation.	Simple or brief connection made between article and class material. Attempts to tell thoughts about the article. Lacks thoughtful ideas that relate to the article. Only one question present and/or are not applicable.	Attempt made to relate article content to class material. Response is inappropriate to the content of the article. Questions attempted.	No response written.
Conventions	Writer makes little or no errors in grammar or spelling that distract the reader from the content. Paragraphs contain sentences that are well-constructed. There are varied beginnings and rich and appropriate vocabulary.	Writer makes very few errors in grammar or spelling that distract the reader from the content. Most sentences are well-constructed with varied beginnings and vocabulary.	Writer makes some major errors in grammar or spelling. Some sentences may not be well-constructed. Similar words are used too often.	Writer makes many errors in grammar or spelling. Sentences lack structure and appear incomplete or are confusing.	No writing submitted or is illegible.
Comments				Total	_____ / 12 pts

CHAPTER 10

FLIGHT MANEUVERS

CONTENTS

Check off each activity upon completion.

LESSON 1

FUNDAMENTAL MANEUVERS: STRAIGHT-AND-LEVEL FLIGHT, CLIMBS, DESCENTS, TURNS

ACTIVITY 1: Fundamental Maneuvers Worksheet

Fly the following maneuvers in the flight simulator and then answer the questions about which flight instruments you are looking at and why.

Straight-and-Level Flight

_____3,000 feet, 100 knots, 060° heading

1. What flight instruments are you looking at to verify that you are level at 3,000 feet, and are at 100 knots on a heading of 060°?

_____

_____

_____

Level Turn

_____3,000 feet, 100 knots, turn right from 090 to 270 degrees

_____3,000 feet, 100 knots, turn left from 270 to 090 degrees

2. What flight instruments are you looking at to verify the 3,000 feet and 100 knots and that you are in a turn?

_____

_____

_____

Straight Climb

_____Heading of 360 degrees, from 3,000 feet to 4,000 feet, 80 knots

3. What flight instruments are you looking at to verify the 80 knots on a heading of 360° and that you are in a climb?

_____

_____

_____

Straight Climb

_____ Heading of 360 degrees, from 4,000 feet to 5,000 feet, 500 fpm

4. What flight instruments are you looking at to verify you are on a heading of 360° and in a climb at 500 fpm going to 5,000 feet?

_____

_____

_____

Straight Descent

_____ Heading of 330 degrees, from 4,000 feet to 3,000 feet, 100 knots

5. What flight instruments are you looking at to verify the 100 knots on a heading of 330° and that you are in a descent?

_____

_____

_____

Straight Descent

_____ Heading of 360 degrees, from 3,000 feet to 2,000 feet, 90 knots

6. What flight instruments are you looking at to verify the 90 knots on a heading of 360° and that you are in a descent?

_____

_____

_____

Turning Climb

_____ Heading of 270 degrees to 090, from 3,500 feet to 4,500 feet, 80 knots

7. What flight instruments are you looking at to verify that you are at 80 knots in a turn and in a climb?

_____

_____

_____

LESSON 2

NORMAL TAKEOFFS AND NORMAL LANDINGS

ACTIVITY 1: Normal Takeoff Thoughts

Aircraft to be used: _____

Rotation speed: _____

Lift-off speed: _____

Flaps: _____

After performing three takeoffs, record two thoughts on your performance of a normal takeoff in the box below.

ACTIVITY 2: Normal Takeoff Completion

_____Completion of a normal takeoff (Facilitator's initials)

Comments on how to improve the normal takeoff: _____

_____

_____

_____

ACTIVITY 3: Normal Landing Thoughts

Flaps: _____

Final/approach speed: _____

After performing three landings, record two thoughts on your performance in the box below.

```



```

ACTIVITY 4: Normal Landing Completion

_____ Completion of a normal landing (Facilitator's initials)

Comments on how to improve the normal landing: _____

_____

_____

_____

LESSON 3

SHORT-FIELD TAKEOFF AND LANDING

ACTIVITY 1: Short-Field Takeoff Thoughts

Aircraft to be used: _____

Rotation speed: _____

Lift-off speed: _____

Flaps: _____

After performing three short-field takeoffs, record two thoughts on your performance in the box below.

ACTIVITY 2: Short-Field Takeoff Completion

_____ Completion of a short-field takeoff (Facilitator's initials)

Comments on how to improve the short-field takeoff: _____

_____

_____

_____

ACTIVITY 3: Short-Field Landings Thoughts

Flaps: _____

Final/approach speed: _____

After performing three short-field landings, record two thoughts on your performance in the box below.

ACTIVITY 4: Short-Field Landings Completion

_____ Completion of a short-field landing (Facilitator's initials)

Comments on how to improve the short-field landing: _____

_____

_____

_____

LESSON 4

SOFT-FIELD TAKEOFF AND LANDING

ACTIVITY 1: Pre-Flight Preparation List

In the space below, list several different things you need to consider before taking off (pre-flight preparation) on a grass runway versus a paved runway.

_____

_____

_____

_____

_____

_____

ACTIVITY 2: Soft-Field Takeoff Thoughts

Aircraft to be used: _____

Rotation speed: _____

Lift-off speed: _____

Flaps: _____

After performing three soft-field takeoffs, record two thoughts on your performance in the box below.

ACTIVITY 3: Soft-Field Takeoff Completion

_____ Completion of a soft-field takeoff (Facilitator's initials)

Comments on how to improve the soft-field takeoff: _____

_____

_____

_____

ACTIVITY 4: Soft-Field Landing Thoughts

Flaps: _____

Final/approach speed: _____

After performing three soft-field landings, record two thoughts on your performance in the box below.

ACTIVITY 5: Soft-Field Landing Completion

_____ Completion of a soft-field landing (Facilitator's initials)

Comments on how to improve the soft-field landing: _____

_____

_____

_____

LESSON 5

STALLS: POWER-ON AND POWER-OFF

ACTIVITY 1: Stalling Video Review

Review the video shown by your facilitator. In the space below, write down why you think the aircraft stalled.

_____

_____

_____

_____

_____

_____

ACTIVITY 2: Power-Off and Power-On Stall Procedures

Aircraft Type: _____

Stall Speed: Clean Configuration: _____

        Dirty (gear and flaps out): _____

Power-Off Stall

Setup and Entry Procedures:

_____

_____

Indication of a stall:

_____

Recovery Procedures:

_____

_____

_____

_____

Power-On Stall

Setup and Entry Procedures:

_____

_____

Indication of a stall:

_____

Recovery Procedures:

_____

_____

_____

_____

ACTIVITY 3: Conducting Power-Off and Power-On Stalls

Power-Off Stall

- How did the stall go?

  _____

  _____

  _____

- In this simulation, what was your first indication that your aircraft was stalling?

  _____

  _____

Power-On Stall

- How did the stall go?

  _____

  _____

  _____

- In this simulation, what was your first indication that your aircraft was stalling?

  _____

  _____

Conducting Power-Off and Power-On Stalls with a Different Aircraft

Aircraft Type: _____

Similarities:

_____

_____

_____

Differences:

_____

_____

_____

Stalling Thoughts

After performing three stalls, record two thoughts on your performance in the box below.

```
┌─────────────────────────────────────────────────────┐
│                                                       │
│                                                       │
│                                                       │
│                                                       │
│                                                       │
│                                                       │
│                                                       │
│                                                       │
│                                                       │
└─────────────────────────────────────────────────────┘
```

ACTIVITY 4: Stall Summary Question

The angle of attack at which an airplane wing stalls will remain the same regardless of gross weight. Why?

_____

_____

_____

_____

_____

LESSON 6

STEEP TURNS

ACTIVITY 1: Steep Turn Procedures

Aircraft Type _____

Maneuver Speed: _____

Review: What flight instrument will tell the pilot what angle of bank the turn is at?

_____

Describe how to perform the steep turn:

_____

_____

_____

Why should the pilot use trim?

_____

_____

_____

ACTIVITY 2: Steep Turns Flight Simulation

The *Airplane Flying Handbook* gives a list of common errors. During your first two steep turns, which of these common errors happened to you?

_____

_____

_____

Steep Turn Completion

_____ Successful completion of a steep turn with Private Pilot Airman Certification Standards (ACS) (Facilitator's Initials):

- ±100 feet of entry altitude
- ±10 knots of entry airspeed
- bank ±5 degrees
- roll out on the entry heading ±10 degrees

LESSON 7

FLIGHT BY REFERENCE TO INSTRUMENTS

ACTIVITY 1: Basic Flight by Instruments Outline

Straight-and-Level Flight:

_____

_____

_____

_____

_____

Constant Airspeed Climbs and Descents:

_____

_____

_____

_____

_____

Turns to Headings:

_____

_____

_____

_____

_____

Unusual Attitudes:

_____

_____

_____

_____

_____

ACTIVITY 2: Flight by Reference to Instruments Simulation

After performing three flights by reference to instruments (instrument meteorological conditions), record two thoughts on your performance in the box below.

Flight by Reference to Instruments Completion

_____ Completion of flight by reference to instruments (Facilitator's initials)

Comments on how to improve flight by reference to instruments: _____

_____

_____

_____

_____

_____

_____

CHAPTER 11

AIRSPACE

CONTENTS

Check off each activity upon completion.

LESSON 1

INTRODUCTION TO AIRSPACE: CONTROLLED VS. UNCONTROLLED

ACTIVITY 1: PHAK Chapter Outline

Take notes of Chapter 15 in the *Pilot's Handbook of Aeronautical Knowledge* as the facilitator conducts an interactive lecture. Be sure to list classifications of airspaces within each category.

1. Regulatory vs. Non-regulatory

   _____

   _____

2. Controlled Airspace:

   _____

   _____

   _____

   _____

   _____

   _____

   _____

   _____

3. Uncontrolled Airspace

   _____

   _____

4. Special Use:

   _____

   _____

   _____

   _____

   _____

   _____

5. Other airspace areas:

_____

_____

_____

ACTIVITY 2: Class A and B Airspace Graphic Organizer

	Class A Airspace	Class B Airspace
Drawing of airspace profile/ structure		
Flight visibility		
Distance from clouds		
Equipment requirements		
Pilot requirements		

LESSON 2

CLASS C, D, AND E AIRSPACE

ACTIVITY 1: Class C, D, and E Airspace Graphic Organizer

	Class C Airspace	Class D Airspace	Class E Airspace
Drawing of airspace profile/ structure			
Flight visibility			Less than 10,000 ft. MSL: At or above 10,000 ft. MSL:
Distance from clouds			Less than 10,000 ft. MSL: At or above 10,000 ft. MSL:
Equipment requirements			
Pilot requirements			

ACTIVITY 2: Comprehension Questions

Answer the following comprehension questions on airspace.

1. When above 18,000 feet MSL, what airspace are you in?

    _____

2. What are the altimeters set to above 18,000 feet?

    _____

3. Is Class E controlled or uncontrolled airspace?

    _____

4. What is the ceiling or top of Class A airspace?

    _____

5. Class D typically goes up to 2,500 feet AGL.

    a. True

    b. False

6. You need a clearance to enter a Class C airspace.

    a. True

    b. False

7. List one thing that you need to enter a Class B airspace.

    _____

8. What is the difference between a prohibited and a restricted airspace?

    _____

    _____

    _____

    _____

    _____

9. What is the primary class of airspace within a TRSA?

    _____

10. Can you as a VFR pilot fly into an active MOA?

    _____

    _____

LESSON 3

UNCONTROLLED AIRSPACE: CLASS G

ACTIVITY 1: Class G Airspace Graphic Organizer

	Class G Airspace		
	1,200 feet or less above the surface (regardless of MSL altitude)	More than 1,200 feet above the surface but less than 10,000 feet MSL	More than 1,200 feet above the surface and at or above 10,000 feet MSL
Drawing of airspace profile/ structure			
Flight visibility	Day:* Night:*	Day: Night:	
Distance from clouds	Day:* Night:*	Day: Night:	
Equipment requirements			

(continued)

Class G Airspace			
	1,200 feet or less above the surface (regardless of MSL altitude)	More than 1,200 feet above the surface but less than 10,000 feet MSL	More than 1,200 feet above the surface and at or above 10,000 feet MSL
Pilot requirements			

*Except as provided in 14 CFR §91.155(b)

ACTIVITY 2: Airspace Worksheet

Note: All questions for this homework assignment are based on using a Twin Cities sectional chart.

1. You just took off from Bemidji Regional Airport (KBJI). You are at 300 feet AGL. Your *Chart Supplement* indicates the Class E (sfc) hours are in effect. What airspace are you in?

   _____

2. What altitude does that airspace (from question 1) begin and end at?

   _____

   _____

3. You decide to fly to Fosston (KFSE). Your enroute altitude is 4,500 feet. What airspace are you in?

   _____

4. At what altitude does controlled airspace begin over Fosston (KFSE)?

   _____

   _____

5. You are now descending into the traffic pattern at Fosston and are preparing to land. You are now at 500 feet AGL. What airspace are you in?

   _____

6. You are flying from Aberdeen, South Dakota (KABR) to Gettysburg, South Dakota (0D8). You are halfway between the two airports at 4,500 feet. What airspace are you in?

   _____

7. What altitude does that airspace (from question 6) begin and end at?

_____

_____

_____

8. You take off out of KBIS (Bismarck, North Dakota) and tower informs you that the clouds are now at 3,500 feet MSL. What is the highest you can fly without breaking your VFR cloud clearances?

   a. 2,000 feet MSL

   b. 2,500 feet MSL

   c. 3,000 feet MSL

   d. 3,400 feet MSL

9. You are 20 NM NE of KJMS (Jamestown, North Dakota) and center informs you that there is a cloud layer moving in and it is at 6,000 feet MSL. You are currently at 6,500 feet MSL and are starting to see clouds. What altitude should you be at to conform to the VFR weather minimums and flight rules for this area?

   a. 6,500 feet MSL

   b. 7,000 feet MSL

   c. 8,500 feet MSL

LESSON 4

SPECIAL USE AND OTHER AIRSPACE

ACTIVITY 1: Notice to Airmen (NOTAM) Article

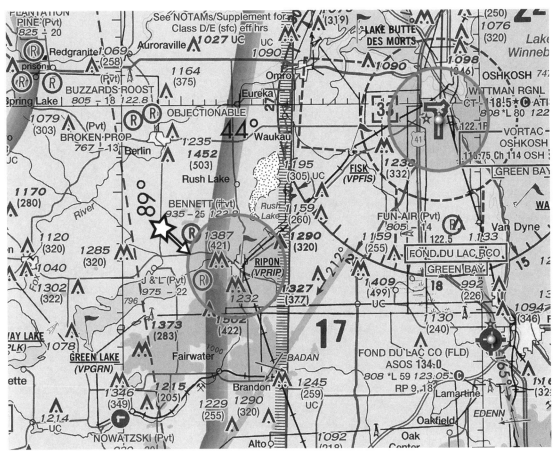

▶ Chart excerpt from NOTAM article. See added star marking the Temporary Flight Restriction (TFR). *(FAA)*

Textual Description of FDC NOTAM: 0/0328

FDC 0/0328 ZAU PART 1 OF 3 WI..AIRSPACE RIPON, WISCONSIN..TEMPORARY FLIGHT RESTRICTIONS. JULY 17, 2020 LOCAL. PURSUANT TO 49 USC 40103(B)(3), THE FEDERAL AVIATION ADMINISTRATION (FAA) CLASSIFIES THE AIRSPACE DEFINED IN THIS NOTAM AS 'NATIONAL DEFENSE AIRSPACE'. PILOTS WHO DO NOT ADHERE TO THE FOLLOWING PROCEDURES MAY BE INTERCEPTED, DETAINED AND INTERVIEWED BY LAW ENFORCEMENT/ SECURITY PERSONNEL. ANY OF THE FOLLOWING ADDITIONAL ACTIONS MAY ALSO BE TAKEN AGAINST A PILOT WHO DOES NOT COMPLY WITH THE REQUIREMENTS OR ANY SPECIAL INSTRUCTIONS OR PROCEDURES ANNOUNCED IN THIS NOTAM: A) THE FAA MAY TAKE ADMINISTRATIVE ACTION, INCLUDING IMPOSING CIVIL PENALTIES AND THE SUSPENSION OR REVOCATION OF AIRMEN CERTIFICATES; OR B) THE UNITED STATES GOVERNMENT MAY PURSUE CRIMINAL CHARGES, INCLUDING CHARGES UNDER TITLE 49 OF THE UNITED STATES CODE, SECTION 46307; OR C) THE UNITED STATES GOVERNMENT MAY USE DEADLY FORCE AGAINST THE AIRBORNE AIRCRAFT, IF IT IS DETERMINED THAT THE AIRCRAFT POSES AN IMMINENT SECURITY THREAT. PURSUANT TO TITLE 14, SECTION 91.141 OF THE CODE OF FEDERAL 2007171500-2007171915 END PART 1 OF 3 FDC 0/0328 ZAU PART 2 OF 3 WI.. AIRSPACE RIPON, WISCONSIN..TEMPORARY FLIGHT REGULATIONS, AIRCRAFT FLIGHT OPERATIONS, TO INCLUDE REMOTE CONTROLLED AIRCRAFT OPERATIONS ARE PROHIBITED: WITHIN AN AREA DEFINED AS 3NM RADIUS OF 435904N0883325W (OSH185000.4) SFC-2999FT AGL EFFECTIVE 2007171500 UTC (1000 LOCAL 07/17/20) UNTIL 2007171615 UTC (1115 LOCAL 07/17/20). WITHIN AN AREA DEFINED AS 3NM RADIUS OF 435039N0885024W (OSH233015.1) SFC-2999FT AGL EFFECTIVE 2007171545 UTC (1045 LOCAL 07/17/20) UNTIL 2007171830 UTC (1330 LOCAL 07/17/20). WITHIN AN AREA DEFINED AS 3NM RADIUS OF 435904N0883325W (OSH185000.4) SFC-2999FT AGL EFFECTIVE 2007171800 UTC (1300 LOCAL 07/17/20) UNTIL 2007171915 UTC (1415 LOCAL 07/17/20). EXCEPT THE FLIGHT OPERATIONS LISTED BELOW: 1. AIRCRAFT ARRIVING OR DEPARTING KOSH AIRPORT. 2007171500-2007171915 END PART 2 OF 3 FDC 0/0328 ZAU PART 3 OF 3 WI..AIRSPACE RIPON, WISCONSIN..TEMPORARY FLIGHT 2. LAW ENFORCEMENT, FIREFIGHTING, AND MEDEVAC/AIR AMBULANCE FLIGHTS ON ACTIVE MISSIONS. 3. AIRCRAFT OPERATIONS NECESSITATED FOR SAFETY OR EMERGENCY REASONS. 4. ALL AIRCRAFT APPROVED TO OPERATE WITHIN THE TFR MUST BE SQUAWKING AN ATC DISCRETE CODE AT ALL TIMES WHILE IN THE TFR AND MUST REMAIN IN TWO-WAY RADIO COMMUNICATIONS WITH ATC. 5. THE SYSTEM OPERATIONS SUPPORT CENTER (SOSC), IS THE POINT OF CONTACT AND COORDINATION FACILITY FOR ANY QUESTIONS REGARDING THIS NOTAM AND ARE AVAILABLE DAILY FROM 0700-2300 EASTERN, PHONE 202-267-8276. 2007171500-2007171915 END PART 3 OF 3

ACTIVITY 2: Airspace Quiz

Note: All questions for this quiz are based on using the Twin Cities sectional chart.

1. You are departing from St. Cloud Regional Airport, Minnesota (KSTC).

   a. What class airspace are you in at 700 feet? _____

   b. What altitude does that airspace start at? _____

   c. What altitude does that airspace end at? _____

2. You are flying to the west towards Sauk Centre (D39) and are halfway between St. Cloud (KSTC) and Sauk Centre at 2,500 feet.

   a. What class airspace are you in? _____

   b. What altitude does that airspace start at? _____

   c. What altitude does that airspace end at? _____

3. You descend into the traffic pattern and are now on final at Sauk Centre at 300 feet AGL.

   a. What class airspace are you in? _____

   b. What altitude does that airspace start at? _____

   c. What altitude does that airspace end at? _____

4. You take off and decide to land at Chandler Field Airport (KAXN) in Alexandria. You fly there and are on final at 300 feet.

   a. What class airspace are you in? _____

   b. What altitude does that airspace start at? _____

   c. What altitude does that airspace end at? _____

5. What is the VFR visibility minimum for Class B airspace?

   a. 1 SM visibility

   b. 3 SM visibility

   c. 5 SM visibility

6. What is the VFR cloud clearance for Class B airspace?

   a. Clear of clouds

   b. 500 feet below the clouds, 1,000 feet above the clouds, and 2,000 feet horizontal

   c. 1,000 feet below the clouds, 1,000 feet above the clouds, and 1 SM horizontal

7. What is the VFR visibility minimum for Class D airspace?

   a. 1 SM visibility

   b. 3 SM visibility

   c. 5 SM visibility

8. What is the VFR cloud clearance for Class D airspace?

   a. Clear of clouds

   b. 500 feet below the clouds, 1,000 feet above the clouds, and 2,000 feet horizontal

   c. 1,000 feet below the clouds, 1,000 feet above the clouds, and 1 SM horizontal

9. What is the VFR visibility minimum for Class E airspace above 10,000 feet?

   a. 1 SM visibility

   b. 3 SM visibility

   c. 5 SM visibility

10. What is the VFR cloud clearance for Class E airspace above 10,000 feet?

   a. Clear of clouds

   b. 500 feet below the clouds, 1,000 feet above the clouds, and 2,000 feet horizontal

   c. 1,000 feet below the clouds, 1,000 feet above the clouds, and 1 SM horizontal

ACTIVITY 3: Special Use and Other Airspace Graphic Organizer

Airspace	Purpose	Pilot Responsibilities for Entry	Time of Use	Altitude
Prohibited Areas				
Restricted Areas				
Warning Areas				
Military Operation Areas (MOAs)				
Alert Areas				
Controlled Firing Areas (CFAs)				
Local Airport Advisory (LAA)				

Airspace	Purpose	Pilot Responsibilities for Entry	Time of Use	Altitude
Military Training Routes (MTRs)				
Temporary Flight Restrictions (TFR)				
Parachute Jump Aircraft Operations				
Published VFR Routes				
Terminal Radar Service Areas (TRSAs)				
National Security Areas (NSAs)				

LESSON 5

REVIEW: AIRSPACE

ACTIVITY 1: Review Study Guide

Note: All questions for this study guide are based on using a Twin Cities sectional chart.

1. What are the pilot requirements to enter Class A airspace?

   _____

2. What are the pilot and equipment requirements to enter a Class B airspace?

   _____

   _____

   _____

   _____

   _____

   _____

   _____

3. You receive the following radio communication from ATC: "SX 22 standby"
   What does this allow you to do when approaching the following airspace:

   a. Class B: _____

   b. Class C: _____

   c. Class D: _____

4. Class G airspace is

   a. Controlled

   b. Uncontrolled

5. Define MSL. _____

6. Define AGL. _____

7. Class D goes up to 2,500 feet AGL.

   a. True

   b. False

8. Two-way radio is required for controlled airspace.

   a. True

   b. False

9. The VFR weather minimums for Class E airspace above 10,000 feet MSL are:

   a. 3 SM visibility; 500 feet below, 1,000 feet above, 2,000 feet horizontal distance from clouds

   b. 5 SM visibility; 1,000 feet below, 1,000 feet above, 1 SM horizontal distance from clouds

   c. 1 SM visibility; clear of clouds

   d. 3 SM visibility; clear of clouds

10. What are the VFR weather minimums for Class A airspace?

    _____

    _____

11. What are the VFR weather minimums for Class B airspace?

    _____

12. What are the VFR weather minimums for Class C airspace?

    _____

    _____

    _____

13. What are the VFR weather minimums for Class D airspace?

    _____

    _____

    _____

14. What are the VFR weather minimums for Class E airspace below 10,000 feet MSL?

    _____

    _____

    _____

15. What are the VFR weather minimums for Class E airspace above 10,000 feet MSL?

    _____

    _____

    _____

16. What are the VFR weather minimums for Class G airspace below 1,200 feet AGL during the day?

_____

_____

17. What are the VFR weather minimums for Class G airspace below 1,200 feet AGL during the night?

_____

_____

_____

18. You are cruising at 6,500 feet MSL in Class E airspace when you notice the bases of the clouds at 6,600 feet MSL. What is the highest altitude you can fly at to maintain your cloud clearance below the clouds?

    a. 6,500 feet MSL

    b. 6,300 feet MSL

    c. 6,100 feet MSL

    d. 5,600 feet MSL

    e. There are no requirements—you just have to stay clear of clouds.

19. What does TFR stand for?

_____

20. Give an example of a TFR?

_____

_____

_____

21. What is the difference between a prohibited area and a restricted area?

_____

_____

_____

_____

_____

_____

22. What altitude does the R-5402 start and end at?

_____

_____

23. What altitude does the Prohibited Area P-204 start and end at?

_____

_____

24. What is an MOA?

_____

_____

25. As a VFR pilot, can you fly into an active MOA?

_____

26. What altitude does that Devils Lake West MOA start and end at?

_____

_____

27. When planning a flight through a TRSA, do you have to have contact with ATC? Why or why not?

_____

_____

_____

28. What class airspace is the primary airport within a TRSA?

_____

29. What does ADIZ stand for?

_____

30. What does the ADIZ mean?

_____

_____

_____

_____

31. You just took off from Thief River Falls airport (KTVF). You are at 300 feet AGL. What airspace are you in?

_____

_____

32. What altitude does that airspace (from question 31) begin *and* end at?

_____

_____

33. You decide to fly to Roseau Municipal Airport (KROX) in Northern Minnesota. Your enroute altitude is 3,500 feet. What airspace are you in?

_____

_____

34. What altitude does that airspace (from question 33) begin *and* end at?

_____

_____

35. About halfway there, you see a note on the sectional that says Thief Lake Wildlife Refuge. How high above the surface should you plan to fly over that wildlife refuge?

_____

_____

36. You are now descending into the traffic pattern at Roseau and are preparing to land. You are now at 500 feet AGL. What airspace are you in?

_____

_____

37. What altitude does that airspace (from question 36) begin *and* end at?

_____

_____

LESSON 6
CHAPTER 11 EXAM

ACTIVITY 1: Article Response and Rubric

Write a one-paragraph response that includes a summary and reflection on the following prompts.

1. Besides being a pilot, what other background or schooling would be beneficial for a hurricane hunter pilot, and why?

2. Describe what a hurricane hunter aircraft and pilot do besides flying into a hurricane.

3. Describe some ways in which you think the hurricane hunter pilots can adjust to the job's demands, long hours, and odd start times, and why is it important that they do so?

Include at least two thoughtful, inquiry-related questions in your reflection. Your response will be graded using the rubric on the next page.

_____

_____

_____

_____

_____

_____

_____

_____

_____

_____

_____

_____

_____

_____

_____

_____

_____

_____

RESPONSE RUBRIC

	Exceeds Expectation (4)	Proficient (3)	Partially Proficient (2)	Novice (1)	Non-Performance (0)
Summary	Information is clearly summarized and demonstrates understanding of the topic. Includes strong supporting details addressing the who, what, where, when, why, and how questions.	Information from source is summarized and general comprehension is demonstrated. Includes supporting details addressing the who, what, where, when, why, and how questions.	Summary may be unclear, incomplete, copies the article, or is inaccurate. There is a need for more supporting details. Summary is only a few sentences.	Summary is vague, too much information was copied from the article, or important details are left out. Details or summary may be confusing.	No summary included.
Reflection	Student is able to relate article content to class material. Insightfully gives personal response with extremely strong thoughts and ideas. Two thoughtful, inquiry related questions are present.	General connection made between article and class material. Tells what their thoughts of the article are, with detail and description. Attempts to push thinking with some prompts. Two questions are submitted that relate to the field of aviation.	Simple or brief connection made between article and class material. Attempts to tell thoughts about the article. Lacks thoughtful ideas that relate to the article. Only one question present and/or are not applicable.	Attempt made to relate article content to class material. Response is inappropriate to the content of the article. Questions attempted.	No response written.
Conventions	Writer makes little or no errors in grammar or spelling that distract the reader from the content. Paragraphs contain sentences that are well-constructed. There are varied beginnings and rich and appropriate vocabulary.	Writer makes very few errors in grammar or spelling that distract the reader from the content. Most sentences are well-constructed with varied beginnings and vocabulary.	Writer makes some major errors in grammar or spelling. Some sentences may not be well-constructed. Similar words are used too often.	Writer makes many errors in grammar or spelling. Sentences lack structure and appear incomplete or are confusing.	No writing submitted or is illegible.

Comments		Total
		_____ / 12 pts

CHAPTER 12

WEATHER

CONTENTS

Check off each activity upon completion.

LESSON 1

WEATHER THEORY (DAY 1)

ACTIVITY 1: Weather Theory Comprehension Questions

Answer the following comprehension questions as your facilitator provides the information during the interactive lecture.

1. Why do pilots need to know about the weather?

2. What causes weather?

3. Which layer of the atmosphere has the greatest impact on flight?

4. What is the difference between atmospheric circulation and atmospheric pressure?

5. Define Coriolis force.

6. How is atmospheric pressure measured?

7. What is a convective current?

_____

_____

8. How might a low-level wind shear impact an aircraft?

_____

_____

_____

9. Define the following atmospheric terms:

   a. Inversion: _____

   _____

   b. Moisture and temperature:_____

   _____

   c. Relative humidity:_____

   _____

   d. Temperature/dew point relationship: _____

   _____

   e. Causes of dew and frost:_____

   _____

   f. Causes of fog:_____

   _____

   g. Causes of clouds:_____

   _____

   h. Ceiling:_____

   _____

   i. Visibility:_____

   _____

   j. Precipitation:_____

   _____

10. Describe the differences among a cold front, warm front, stationary front, and occluded front.

_____

_____

_____

_____

_____

_____

_____

_____

_____

_____

11. Explain how thunderstorms and the associated hazards impact flight.

_____

_____

_____

_____

_____

_____

_____

_____

LESSON 2

WEATHER THEORY (DAY 2)

ACTIVITY 1: Weather Demonstration Notes

Air Pressure and Density Altitude—The Water Glass Trick

The Coriolis Effect—Balloon

Cloud Formation—A Cloud in a Bottle

Air Mass—Lamp, Ice, and a Box

ACTIVITY 2: Reading Assignment Response Questions

Directions: Read the article provided by your facilitator about air safety as it relates to weather and a pilot's background knowledge of weather principles. Using what you know about weather and flight decision-making, answer the following questions.

1. What factors influence atmospheric pressure?

   _____

   _____

   _____

   _____

   _____

   _____

2. Explain at least two ways the pilot could have prevented this accident.

   _____

   _____

   _____

   _____

   _____

   _____

3. What weather principles affected the flight?

   _____

   _____

   _____

   _____

   _____

   _____

4. Explain how one of the principles identified in question #3 works.

   _____

   _____

   _____

   _____

   _____

   _____

LESSON 3

WEATHER PRODUCTS: METAR

ACTIVITY 1: METAR Notes

1. What is a METAR?

   _____

   _____

   _____

   _____

2. How often does it come out?

   _____

3. What information is included in a typical METAR report? Label the following elements of a METAR in the example below by placing the correct letter in the space provided.

   - Type of report _____
   - Station identifier _____
   - Date and time (Zulu time) of report _____
   - Modifier (if included as AUTO, it is an automated station) _____
   - Wind _____

   - Visibility _____
   - Weather _____
   - Sky condition _____
   - Temperature and dew point _____
   - Altimeter setting _____
   - Remarks _____

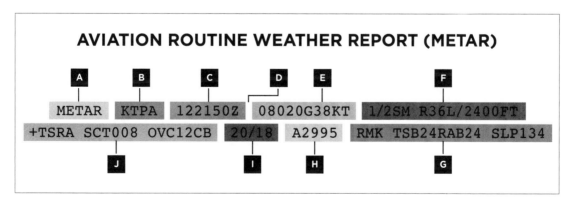

▶ Aviation Routine Weather Report (METAR) elements.

4. Fill in the definitions of the METAR/TAF abbreviations in the table below.

METAR/TAF Abbreviations	
Abbreviation	Definition
SN	
TS	
RA	
FG	
BR	
SH	
BKN	
CLR	
OVC	
FEW	
HZ	
+	
−	

ACTIVITY 2: Decoding METARs

Decode the following METARS.

METAR Example #2:

KGFK 081253Z 28007KT 10SM CLR M01/M02 A3041 RMK AO2 SLP308 T10061022

- Type of report _____
- Station identifier _____
- Date and time (Zulu time) of report _____
- Modifier (if included as AUTO, it is an automated station) _____
- Wind _____
- Visibility _____
- Weather _____
- Sky condition _____
- Temperature and dew point _____
- Altimeter setting _____
- Remarks _____

METAR Example #3:

K40J 021835Z AUTO 29007KT 3SM +RA SCT008 BKN018 OVC046 24/23 A3008
RMK AO2 LTG DSNT E THRU SW P0031 T02350228

- Type of report _____
- Station identifier _____
- Date and time (Zulu time) of report _____
- Modifier (if included as AUTO, it is an automated station) _____
- Wind _____
- Visibility _____
- Weather _____
- Sky condition _____
- Temperature and dew point _____
- Altimeter setting _____
- Remarks _____

METAR Example #4:

K2J3 021835Z AUTO 09004KT 2 1/2SM -TSRA BR SCT031 SCT050 BKN090 24/24 A3006 RMK AO2 LTG DSNT NE E AND SW P0013 T02440239

- Type of report _____

- Station identifier _____

- Date and time (Zulu time) of report _____

- Modifier (if included as AUTO, it is an automated station) _____

- Wind _____

- Visibility _____

- Weather _____

- Sky condition _____

- Temperature and dew point _____

- Altimeter setting _____

- Remarks _____

METAR Example #5:

KLAX 081253Z 11003KT 10SM FEW006 FEW200 14/12 A3005 RMK AO2 SLP174 T01440122 $

- Type of report _____

- Station identifier _____

- Date and time (Zulu time) of report _____

- Modifier (if included as AUTO, it is an automated station) _____

- Wind _____

- Visibility _____

- Weather _____

- Sky condition _____

- Temperature and dew point _____

- Altimeter setting _____

- Remarks _____

METAR Example #6:

KFMH 270535Z AUTO 03032G52KT 1/4SM SN OVC002 M01/M02 A2955 RMK A02

- Type of report _____

- Station identifier _____

- Date and time (Zulu time) of report _____

- Modifier (if included as AUTO, it is an automated station) _____

- Wind _____

- Visibility _____

- Weather _____

- Sky condition _____

- Temperature and dew point _____

- Altimeter setting _____

- Remarks _____

ACTIVITY 3: METARs Worksheet

KBIS 171352Z 14007KT 9SM OVC011 M10/M12 A3028 RMK AO2 SNB14E41 SLP289
P0000 T11001122

1. What is the temperature for KBIS? _____

2. What are the winds for KBIS? _____

3. What is the visibility for KBIS? _____

KGFK 171353Z 30004KT 10SM CLR M18/M21 A3037 RMK AO2 SLP311 T11831206

4. What is the sky condition at KGFK? _____

5. What is the dew point at KGFK? _____

KEGV 171355Z AUTO 30007KT 2 1/2SM -SN SCT015 SCT021 OVC028 M09/M10
A3010 RMK AO2 T10881101

6. What is the ceiling at KEVG? _____

7. What type of precipitation is falling at KEVG? _____

8. What is the intensity of that precipitation? _____

KOSH 171353Z 29015G18KT 10SM OVC022 M04/M09 A3017 RMK AO2 SLP234
T10441089

9. What are the winds at KOSH? _____

10. What is the altimeter setting at KOSH? _____

11. What is the ceiling for KOSH? _____

KCRP 171416Z 00000KT 1 1/2SM +RA BR SCT009 OVC015 16/15 A3015 RMK AO2
TWR VIS 1 3/4 P0006 T01610150

12. What are the winds at KCRP today? _____

13. What type of precipitation is occurring at KCRP today? _____

14. What is the intensity of that precipitation? _____

KSPL 171355Z AUTO 05007KT 3/4SM VV005 A3013 RMK AO1 VSBY 1/2V3

15. What day and time was the METAR for KSPL issued? _____

16. What does the AUTO mean? _____

17. What does the VV005 mean? _____

KRHP 171355Z AUTO 00000KT 1/4SM FZFG OVC001 M01/M01 A3019 RMK AO2
T10141014

18. What is the precipitation that is occurring at KRHP? _____

19. What is the ceiling at KRHP? _____

20. What is the visibility for KRHP? _____

LESSON 4

WEATHER PRODUCTS: TAF

ACTIVITY 1: TAF Notes

1. What is a TAF?

   _____

   _____

   _____

   _____

2. What does TAF stand for?

   _____

   _____

3. How often does it come out?

   _____

   _____

4. What information is included in a typical TAF report?

   _____

   _____

   _____

   _____

   _____

   _____

   _____

   _____

TAF Example #1:

```
MSP 241740Z 2418/2524 13013G21KT P6SM OVC018
    FM241930 13012G19KT 5SM -SHRA BR SCT008 OVC020
    TEMPO 2420/2422 1 1/2SM -SHRA BR OVC008
    FM250100 21010KT 5SM BR SCT020 OVC040
    FM250800 25012KT P6SM OVC015 PROB30 2510/2516 -SHSN
    FM251600 25015G23KT P6SM OVC035=
```

- Type of report _____

- ICAO station identifier _____

- Date and time of origin _____

- Valid period dates and times _____

- Forecast wind _____

- Forecast visibility _____

- Forecast significant weather _____

- Forecast sky condition _____

- Forecast change group _____

- Probability group _____

ACTIVITY 2: Decoding TAFs

Decode the following TAFs.

TAF Example #2:

```
KINL 201149Z 2012/2112 27012G20KT P6SM -SN BKN018 OVC025
    TEMPO 2012/2016 4SM -SN BR OVC012
    FM201900 28013G20KT P6SM VCSH BKN025 OVC040
    FM210100 28009KT P6SM SCT025 BKN050
    FM210600 29008KT P6SM VCSH OVC015
```

- Type of report _____

- ICAO station identifier _____

- Date and time of origin _____

- Valid period dates and times _____

- Forecast wind _____

- Forecast visibility _____

- Forecast significant weather _____

- Forecast sky condition _____

- Forecast change group _____

- Probability group _____

TAF Example #3:

```
KGFK 201120Z 2012/2112 27008KT P6SM SKC
   FM201700 30010KT P6SM SCT030
   FM210000 27006KT P6SM SKC
```

- Type of report _____

- ICAO station identifier _____

- Date and time of origin _____

- Valid period dates and times _____

- Forecast wind _____

- Forecast visibility _____

- Forecast significant weather _____

- Forecast sky condition _____

- Forecast change group _____

- Probability group _____

TAF Example #4:

```
TAF AMD CYQM 201141Z 2012/2112 10005KT P6SM BKN020
   TEMPO 2012/2101 SCT020 OVC130
   BECMG 2014/2016 15015G25KT
   FM210100 14015G25KT P6SM -RA SCT008 OVC020
   FM210500 13012KT 5SM -RA BR OVC012
   PROB30 2105/2110 2SM RA BR OVC003
   FM211000 19010KT P6SM BKN040
   BECMG 2110/2112 29010KT
```

- Type of report _____

- ICAO station identifier _____

- Date and time of origin _____

- Valid period dates and times _____

- Forecast wind _____

- Forecast visibility _____

- Forecast significant weather _____

- Forecast sky condition _____

- Forecast change group _____

- Probability group _____

ACTIVITY 3: TAF Homework

Decode the following TAFs:

```
KINL 091142Z 0912/1012 21004KT P6SM SKC
   FM091700 22010G15KT P6SM SKC
   FM100000 22008KT P6SM SCT200 WS020/25040KT
   FM100900 24006KT P6SM SCT200
```

- Type of report _____

- ICAO station identifier _____

- Date and time of origin _____

- Valid period dates and times _____

- Forecast wind _____

- Forecast visibility _____

- Forecast significant weather _____

- Forecast sky condition _____

- Forecast change group _____

- Probability group _____

```
TAF KRDR 091000Z 0910/1016 23009KT 9999 FEW250 QNH2988INS WND
20012KT AFT 0916
   BECMG 1015/1016 33012G18KT 9999 FEW200 QNH3003INS TX15/0921Z
   TN05/0912Z
```

- Type of report _____

- ICAO station identifier _____

- Date and time of origin _____

- Valid period dates and times _____

- Forecast wind _____

- Forecast visibility _____

- Forecast significant weather _____

- Forecast sky condition _____

- Forecast change group _____

- Probability group _____

```
TAF CYQM 091138Z 0912/1012 23008KT P6SM BKN220
   BECMG 0912/0914 28009KT
   FM092100 27007KT P6SM SCT020 BKN100
   FM092300 29008KT P6SM -SHRA OVC015
   BECMG 0923/1001 35010G20KT
   FM100200 30010G20KT P6SM OVC020
   FM101100 29009KT P6SM BKN030 RMK NXT FCST BY 091800Z
```

- Type of report _____

- ICAO station identifier _____

- Date and time of origin _____

- Valid period dates and times _____

- Forecast wind _____

- Forecast visibility _____

- Forecast significant weather _____

- Forecast sky condition _____

- Forecast change group _____

- Probability group _____

LESSON 5

WEATHER PRODUCTS: AIRMETS AND SIGMETS

ACTIVITY 1: AIRMET & SIGMET Notes

AIRMET

- What is an AIRMET?

  _____

- What is the purpose of an AIRMET?

  _____

  _____

  _____

  _____

- What is the valid time frame of an AIRMET?

  _____

  _____

- What are the three types of AIRMETs?

  _____

  _____

  _____

  _____

  _____

  _____

  _____

  _____

AIRMET Example #1:

```
WAUS44 KKCI 021445
DFWZ WA 021445
AIRMET ZULU UPDT 3 FOR ICE AND FRZLVL VALID UNTIL 022100
AIRMET ICE...TN AL
FROM 40ESE BWG TO HMV TO GQO TO 50SW PZD TO 30W CEW TO 40ESE MEI
TO 40ESE BWG
MOD ICE BTN 140 AND FL300. CONDS CONTG BYD 21Z ENDG BY 03Z.
FRZLVL...RANGING FROM 130-170 ACRS AREA
    160 ALG 60W INK-80WSW INK-30NW MRF-20ESE MRF-30WSW PSX-70SSE
    PSX-110ENE BRO
```

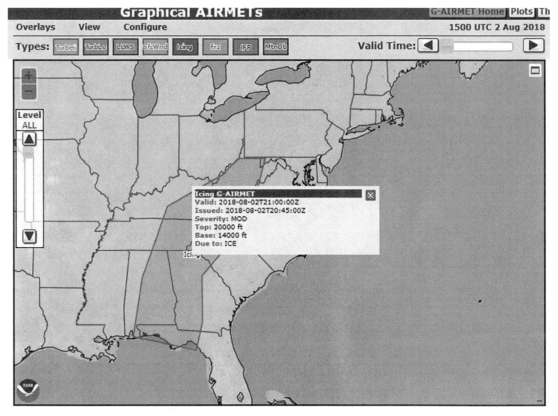

▶ Graphical AIRMET. *(NWS Aviation Weather Center)*

Interpretation:

_____

_____

_____

_____

_____

AIRMET Example #2:

```
WAUS44 KKCI 022045
DFWT WA 022045
AIRMET TANGO UPDT 4 FOR TURB VALID UNTIL 030300
AIRMET TURB...OK TX
FROM 50ESE ADM TO 50WSW TXK TO 60WNW LFK TO 30S CWK TO JCT TO
20E ABI TO 30SW ADM TO 50ESE ADM
MOD TURB BLW 100. CONDS ENDG 00-03Z.
OTLK VALID 0300-0900Z...TURB TX LA MS AND CSTL WTRS
BOUNDED BY 50ENE ABI-40E ACT-40NNW PSX-AEX-30NNW MCB-90WSW LEV-
120SSW LCH-80E BRO-90W BRO-DLF-90S MRF-70WNW MRF-50ENE ABI
MOD TURB BTN FL300 AND FL430. CONDS CONTG THRU 09Z.
```

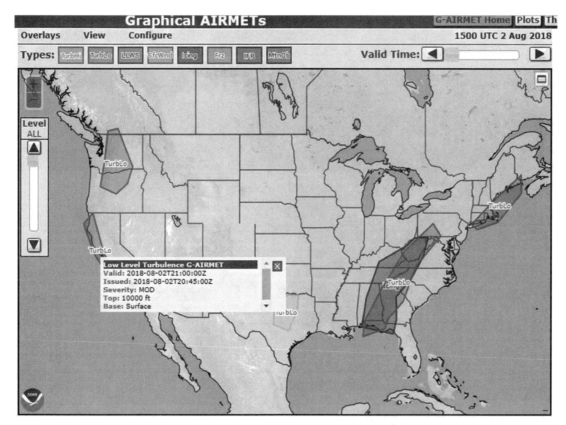

▶ Graphical AIRMET. *(NWS Aviation Weather Center)*

Interpretation:

_____

_____

_____

_____

_____

SIGMET

- What is a SIGMET?

_____

_____

- What is the purpose of a SIGMET?

_____

_____

_____

_____

_____

_____

- What is the valid time frame of an SIGMET?

_____

_____

_____

SIGMET Example #1:

```
WSUS31 KKCI 022055
SIGE
CONVECTIVE SIGMET 06E
VALID UNTIL 2255Z
NC SC FL GA AND FL CSTL WTRS
FROM 40N SPA-30SE CAE-20SSE SRQ-40WSW CTY-30SE ATL-40N SPA
AREA SEV TS MOV FROM 20015KT. TOPS ABV FL450.
TORNADOES...HAIL TO 1 IN...WIND GUSTS TO 50KT POSS.

OUTLOOK VALID 022255-030255
AREA 1...FROM CON-50SSE ECG-60ENE CRG-PBI-70WSW EYW-100WSW
PIE-200SE LEV-SJI-BNA-30NNW EWC-CON
WST ISSUANCES EXPD. REFER TO MOST RECENT ACUS01 KWNS FROM STORM
PREDICTION CENTER FOR SYNOPSIS AND METEOROLOGICAL DETAILS.

AREA 2...FROM 40SSE SSM-30NE ECK-BVT-40NE ORD-40SSE SSM
WST ISSUANCES POSS. REFER TO MOST RECENT ACUS01 KWNS FROM STORM
PREDICTION CENTER FOR SYNOPSIS AND METEOROLOGICAL DETAILS.
```

Interpretation:

_____

_____

_____

_____

_____

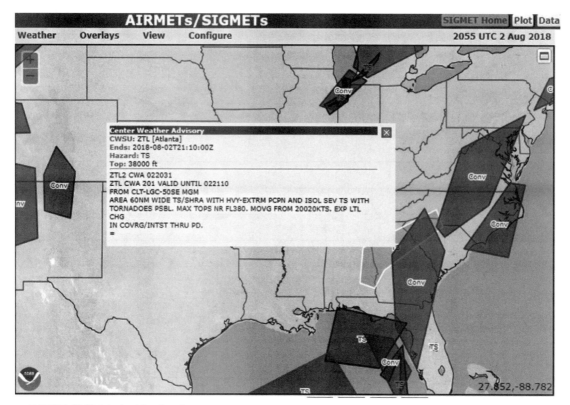

AIRMETs/SIGMETs

Weather   Overlays   View   Configure

SIGMET Home Plot Data

2055 UTC 2 Aug 2018

Center Weather Advisory
CWSU: ZTL [Atlanta]
Ends: 2018-08-02T21:10:00Z
Hazard: TS
Top: 38000 ft

ZTL2 CWA 022031
ZTL CWA 201 VALID UNTIL 022110
FROM CLT-LGC-50SE MGM
AREA 60NM WIDE TS/SHRA WITH HVY-EXTRM PCPN AND ISOL SEV TS WITH
TORNADOES PSBL. MAX TOPS NR FL380. MOVG FROM 20020KTS. EXP LTL
CHG
IN COVRG/INTST THRU PD.
=

27.852,-88.782

▶ SIGMET. *(NWS Aviation Weather Center)*

SIGMET Example #2:

```
WSUS32 KKCI 022055
SIGC
CONVECTIVE SIGMET 42C
VALID UNTIL 2255Z
MI IN IL LM
FROM 30W PMM-30ENE GIJ-30W BVT-50SSW JOT-30W PMM
AREA TS MOV FROM 23025KT. TOPS ABV FL450.

OUTLOOK VALID 022255-030255
AREA 1...FROM 40WNW PMM-BVT-60S AXC-30ESE UIN-40WNW PMM
WST ISSUANCES POSS. REFER TO MOST RECENT ACUS01 KWNS FROM STORM
PREDICTION CENTER FOR SYNOPSIS AND METEOROLOGICAL DETAILS.

AREA 2...FROM 50N CHE-40SSE CYS-70NW AMA-CME-30NE TCS-50N CHE
WST ISSUANCES POSS. REFER TO MOST RECENT ACUS01 KWNS FROM STORM
PREDICTION CENTER FOR SYNOPSIS AND METEOROLOGICAL DETAILS.
```

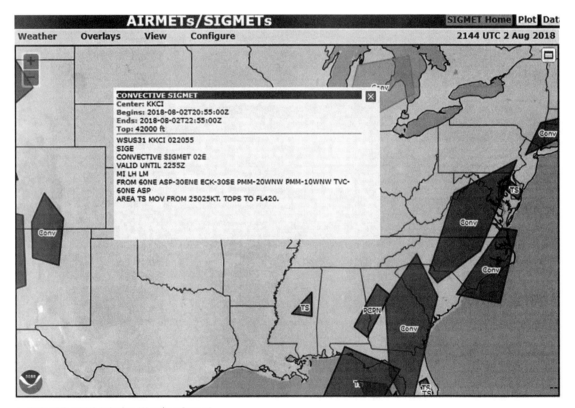

▶ SIGMET. *(NWS Aviation Weather Center)*

Interpretation:

_____

_____

_____

_____

_____

Winds & Temperature Aloft Charts

- What is a Winds and Temperature Aloft chart?

  _____

  _____

  _____

  _____

- What is its purpose?

  _____

  _____

  _____

  _____

  _____

- How often are they available?

  _____

  _____

```
DATA BASED ON 020000Z
VALID 020600Z    FOR USE 0200-0900Z. TEMPS NEG ABV 24000

FT  3000     6000     9000    12000    18000    24000   30000   34000   39000
BRL 2424 2721+14 2610+09 3017+01 2916-12 2815-24 331340 331150 262151
DBQ 2519 2523+13 2626+07 2724+01 2822-12 2818-23 281840 281650 272754
DSM 3509 2721+14 2924+09 3031+02 3122-12 3123-23 312340 312649 323352
MCW 3613 2815+10 2919+09 3021+03 3125-11 3027-23 312840 312350 322854
JOT 2420 2716+13 2611+07 2815+00 2716-12 2617-24 232540 223349 233852
SPI 2413 2914+14 3107+08 3410+01 2912-12 2513-24 232040 222448 232851
EVV 9900 9900+12 3405+07 9900+04 2309-10 2321-23 223539 215046 216552
FWA 2510 2506+12 2605+06 2809+01 2718-11 2522-22 233538 226046 228454
IND 2505 2905+12 9900+07 3006+02 2515-10 2318-23 233638 225046 216953
GCK      1914+18 0110+14 3318+08 3328-09 3337-19 325235 325546 325954
GLD      1818    2711+14 3111+07 3220-09 3331-20 334536 325646 325854
```

▶ Winds and Temperature Aloft Forecast _(NWS Aviation Weather Center)_

Prognostic Charts

- What is a prognostic chart?

_____

_____

- What is its purpose?

_____

_____

_____

_____

- How often are they available?

_____

_____

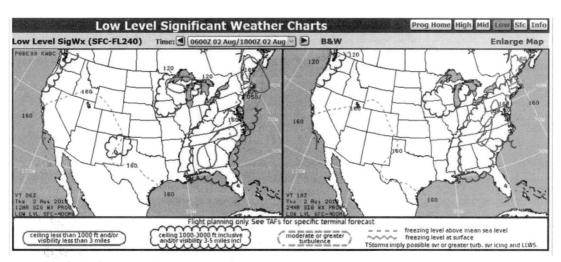

▸ Low-Level Significant Weather Prognostic Chart. *(NWS Aviation Weather Center)*

ACTIVITY 2: Prognostic Chart Summary Forecast

Summarize the weather forecast from the Prognostic Chart shown below.

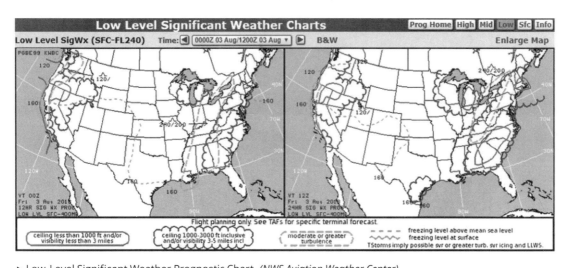

▶ Low-Level Significant Weather Prognostic Chart. *(NWS Aviation Weather Center)*

_____

_____

_____

_____

_____

_____

_____

_____

_____

_____

LESSON 6

WEATHER-RELATED DECISION MAKING

ACTIVITY 1: Go/No-Go Decision Scenarios

PAVE Checklist:

P _____

A _____

V _____

E _____

Make the decision as a pilot to take the flight (Go) or not take the flight (No Go) based on your knowledge of weather and the PAVE Environment considerations for each scenario (See *Pilot's Handbook of Aeronautical Knowledge,* Chapter 2). Make sure to consider the terminal airport weather as well as any route hazards.

Weather-related prompts to consider:

1. What is the current ceiling and visibility? In mountainous terrain, consider having higher minimums for ceiling and visibility, particularly if the terrain is unfamiliar.

2. Consider the possibility that the weather may be different than forecast. Have alternative plans and be ready and willing to divert, should an unexpected change occur.

3. Consider the winds at the airports being used and the strength of the crosswind component.

4. If flying in mountainous terrain, consider whether there are strong winds aloft. Strong winds in mountainous terrain can cause severe turbulence and downdrafts and be very hazardous for aircraft even when there is no other significant weather.

5. Are there any thunderstorms present or forecast?

6. If there are clouds, is there any icing, current or forecast? What is the temperature/dew point spread and the current temperature at altitude? Can descent be made safely all along the route?

7. If icing conditions are encountered, is the pilot experienced at operating the aircraft's deicing or anti-icing equipment? Is this equipment in good condition and functional? For what icing conditions is the aircraft rated, if any?

Scenario Reference Information

Below are the weather reports and information you will need to refer to for the scenarios that follow.

Scenario 1

METAR:

```
KABQ 290352Z 01016KT 10SM CLR 06/M11 A3043 RMK AO2 SLP306 T00561111
```

Scenario 2

Current date and time:

```
Zulu (UTC)      29-Jan-2018 04:53:31
Local (UTC-6)   28-Jan-2018 22:53:31
```

METARs:

```
KOMA 290352Z 34013KT 10SM CLR M09/M13 A3060 RMK AO2 SLP379
T10941133
KFSD  290356Z 28003KT 10SM CLR M16/M18 A3062 RMK AO2 SLP405
T11611178
```

TAFs:

```
KOMA 290349Z 2904/2924 35013KT P6SM BKN070 SCT100
  TEMPO 2907/2910 BKN020
  FM291000 35009KT P6SM FEW020 SCT250 FM291400 34005KT P6SM SCT250


KFSD 282322Z 2823/2924 36007KT P6SM FEW100
  FM291100 VRB03KT P6SM SCT200
```

Winds and Temperature Aloft Forecast:

```
TEMPS NEG ABV 24000
FT   3000 6000     9000     12000   18000    24000    30000   34000   39000
OMA 1027 1326+01  1428-03  1431-09 1639-21  1749-34  175849  175957  174758
FSD       2849+04 2857-02  2760-07 2670-20  2682-32  760344  760648  259451
```

Scenario 5

▶ Radar Summary Chart.
(aviationweather.gov)

Scenario	Decision: Go or No-Go?	Rationale with supporting evidence from weather theory and PAVE
1. You are departing Albuquerque International Airport in New Mexico (KABQ). Go to **airnav.com/airports/** and type in KABQ to view airport information, including runway available. You have pre-flighted your aircraft and you are ready to depart. You obtain the local weather METAR (see above). Based on this weather information, how would this affect your decision to Go or Not-to-Go? Why?		
2. You are departing Eppley Airfield in Omaha Nebraska (KOMA) going to Joe Foss Field in Sioux Falls, SD (KFSD). Go to **airnav.com/airports/** and type in KOMA and KFSD to view airport information, including field elevation. Review the METARs, TAFs, and Winds Aloft forecast (see above). Based on the weather information, with a departure in 30 minutes from the current date and time, what is your Go or No-Go decision? If you are going, based on the weather, what altitude do you plan on using for your route of flight?		

Scenario	Decision: Go or No-Go?	Rationale with supporting evidence from weather theory and PAVE
3. You are departing Fort Collins-Loveland Municipal Airport (KFNL) in Fort Collins, Colorado. You are heading to Cheyenne Regional Airport in Cheyenne, WY (KCYS). Go to **airnav.com/airports/** and type in KFNL and KCYS to view airport information, including field elevation. It is January and the temperature is 20°F, there are clouds at 5,000 feet, and there are reports of scattered snow showers. How would this affect your Go or No-Go decision? What could be a hazard of flying this route?		
4. Today's temperature is going to be 100°F. If you are going on a flight, what altitude would you choose to avoid convective turbulence: 3,000 feet or 6,000 feet? If these weather conditions warranted the creation of an AIRMET Tango, how would this affect your Go or No-Go decision?		
5. You are planning a flight from Miami, Florida to Orlando, Florida. Review the current radar reports (see above). How would this affect your Go or No-Go decision? What concerns do you have regarding going in these weather conditions?		

LESSON 7

REVIEW: WEATHER

ACTIVITY 1: Review Questions Brainstorming

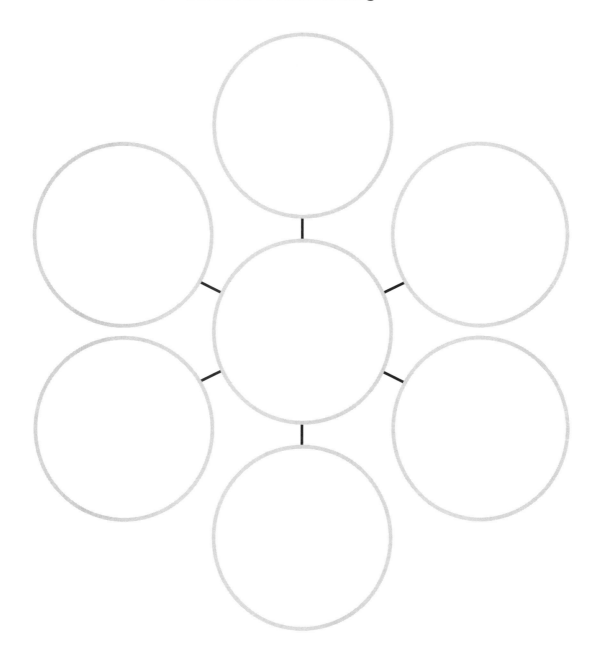

LESSON 8

CHAPTER 12 EXAM

ACTIVITY 1: Article Response and Rubric

Article Response

1. Complete the four-question automated quiz with the article on Newsela.

2. Write a two-paragraph response that includes an article summary and reflection on the following prompts:

   - How could the hypoxia experienced by the mountain climbers impact a pilot and flight safety?

   - Explain the impact/importance of a pilot's health and understanding of physiological factors on flight performance.

Include at least two thoughtful, inquiry-related questions in your reflection. Your response will be graded using the rubric provided on the next page.

_____

_____

_____

_____

_____

_____

_____

_____

_____

_____

_____

_____

_____

_____

_____

_____

RESPONSE RUBRIC

	Exceeds Expectation (4)	Proficient (3)	Partially Proficient (2)	Novice (1)	Non-Performance (0)
Summary	Information is clearly summarized and demonstrates understanding of the topic. Includes strong supporting details addressing the who, what, where, when, why, and how questions.	Information from source is summarized and general comprehension is demonstrated. Includes supporting details addressing the who, what, where, when, why, and how questions.	Summary may be unclear, incomplete, copies the article, or is inaccurate. There is a need for more supporting details. Summary is only a few sentences.	Summary is vague, too much information was copied from the article, or important details are left out. Details or summary may be confusing.	No summary included.
Reflection	Student is able to relate article content to class material. Insightfully gives personal response with extremely strong thoughts and ideas. Two thoughtful, inquiry related questions are present.	General connection made between article and class material. Tells what their thoughts of the article are, with detail and description. Attempts to push thinking with some prompts. Two questions are submitted that relate to the field of aviation.	Simple or brief connection made between article and class material. Attempts to tell thoughts about the article. Lacks thoughtful ideas that relate to the article. Only one question present and/or are not applicable.	Attempt made to relate article content to class material. Response is inappropriate to the content of the article. Questions attempted.	No response written.
Conventions	Writer makes little or no errors in grammar or spelling that distract the reader from the content. Paragraphs contain sentences that are well-constructed. There are varied beginnings and rich and appropriate vocabulary.	Writer makes very few errors in grammar or spelling that distract the reader from the content. Most sentences are well-constructed with varied beginnings and vocabulary.	Writer makes some major errors in grammar or spelling. Some sentences may not be well-constructed. Similar words are used too often.	Writer makes many errors in grammar or spelling. Sentences lack structure and appear incomplete or are confusing.	No writing submitted or is illegible.

Comments | | | **Total** _____ / 12 pts

CHAPTER 13

AEROMEDICAL FACTORS

CONTENTS

Check off each activity upon completion.

LESSON 1

IMSAFE CHECKLIST

ACTIVITY 1: Before Graphic Organizer

Your facilitator will read these statements to you before you begin Chapter 13, and you will check "Agree" if you agree with the statement or "Disagree" if you disagree with the statement. At the close of Chapter 13, you will revisit this activity and again state whether you agree or disagree with the statements.

Statement	Agree	Disagree
If you want an aviation medical, go see a medical doctor.		
You should not fly if you are taking any medication.		
The Federal Aviation Regulations require 8 hours between drinking and flying.		
The effects of hypoxia can occur at low altitudes.		
Hyperventilation is when your body expels too much oxygen.		
Carbon monoxide poisoning is a real concern for pilots while flying.		
Ear blocks are more painful when climbing than descending.		
A somatogravic illusion is due to slow bank.		
The parts of your eyes that you use at night are called the cones.		

ACTIVITY 2: IMSAFE Acronym

I	
M	
S	
A	
F	
E	

LESSON 2

HYPOXIA AND HYPERVENTILATION

ACTIVITY 1: Guided Notes

1. Hypoxia is the lack of _____ to the body.

2. What are the four types of hypoxia? What are characteristics of each type?

   _____
   _____
   _____
   _____
   _____
   _____

3. What are the symptoms of hypoxia?

   _____
   _____
   _____
   _____

4. What is the corrective action for hypoxia?

   _____
   _____

5. What is hyperventilation?

   _____
   _____
   _____

6. What are the symptoms of hyperventilation?

   _____
   _____
   _____

7. What is the corrective action for hyperventilation?

_____

_____

ACTIVITY 2: Video Observations

1. While watching the Altitude Chamber Hypoxia Training video, record what you observe about the participants each minute, starting at the beginning. Note: Pay close attention to the different people and their reactions.

   - Minute 0:00 — _____
   - Minute 1:00 — _____
   - Minute 2:00 — _____
   - Minute 3:00 — _____
   - Minute 4:00 — _____
   - Minute 5:00 — _____
   - Minute 6:00 — _____

2. What happened as the time progressed?

_____

_____

3. While watching the centrifuge G-force training video, record what you observe about how the participants look and what happened to their breathing.

_____

_____

_____

_____

_____

4. Why do you think the military requires G-force training?

_____

_____

_____

_____

LESSON 3

OTHER AEROMEDICAL FACTORS

ACTIVITY 1: Illusion Training Graphic Organizer

In the video shown by your facilitator, how have the pilots trained their bodies to handle the illusions? Write your thoughts below.

ACTIVITY 2: Aeromedical Factors Outline

Aeromedical Factor	Definition	Symptoms	Remedy/Reaction
Decompression sickness			
Ear block			
Sinus block			
Toothaches			
Carbon monoxide poisining			
Motion sickness			
Blood donation			
Dehydration			
Oxygen use			

LESSON 4

VISUAL ILLUSIONS

ACTIVITY 1: Illusions Presentations

Presentation Checklist

Use the following checklist when creating your illusions presentation.

Criteria	Points Earned	Total Points
1. List illusion		5 points
2. Define the illusion		5 points
3. Why might a pilot experience this?		5 points
4. How should a pilot learn to avoid this?		5 points
5. Provide visual examples using pictures and/or videos		5 points
Total		25 points

Illusions Presentation Graphic Organizer

Illusion 1	
Definition	
Why might a pilot experience it?	
Avoidance	
Visuals (describe)	

Illusion 2	
Definition	
Why might a pilot experience it?	
Avoidance	
Visuals (describe)	

Illusion 3	
Definition	
Why might a pilot experience it?	
Avoidance	
Visuals (describe)	

Illusion 4	
Definition	
Why might a pilot experience it?	
Avoidance	
Visuals (describe)	

Illusion 5	
Definition	
Why might a pilot experience it?	
Avoidance	
Visuals (describe)	

Illusion 6	
Definition	
Why might a pilot experience it?	
Avoidance	
Visuals (describe)	

LESSON 5

NIGHT FLIGHT

ACTIVITY 1: Differences Between Flying During the Day and at Night

Day Time Flying	Night Time Flying

ACTIVITY 2: Night Flight Video Questions

When watching the night flight video, answer the following questions.

1:17—What color is the light on the flashlight?

_____

_____

2:02—Describe how easy or difficult it is to see the runway.

_____

_____

_____

2:10—What colors are the PAPIs (the four lights on the left side of the runway)?

_____

_____

4:47—How does this touchdown compare to his first?

_____

_____

_____

8:30—What did the student forget to turn on? How did this impact his landing?

_____

_____

_____

ACTIVITY 3: Eyes and Night Vision Questions

Answer the following questions as your facilitator presents the information in class.

1. What do the cones do?

   _____

   _____

2. What do the rods do?

   _____

   _____

3. Where is your night blind spot?

   _____

   _____

4. How should your scan differ between a day flight and night flight?

   _____

   _____

5. How long does it take for your eyes to adjust to the dark?

   _____

   _____

6. How should you adjust your in-flight lighting at night?

   _____

   _____

7. What color flashlight should you use for exterior preflight? Why?

   _____

   _____

8. What color flashlight should you use while in flight? Why?

   _____

   _____

9. If, after preflight, you have to go back inside the FBO to go to the bathroom, how do you save your night vision?

   _____

   _____

LESSON 6

REVIEW: AEROMEDICAL FACTORS

ACTIVITY 1: Vocabulary BINGO

B	I	N	G	O
		free		

ACTIVITY 2: After Graphic Organizer

Your facilitator read these statements to you before you began Chapter 13. Now, at the close of Chapter 13, you will again indicate whether you agree or disagree with the statements by checking the appropriate column.

Statement	Agree	Disagree
If you want an aviation medical, go see a medical doctor.		
You should not fly if you are taking any medication.		
The Federal Aviation Regulations require 8 hours between drinking and flying.		
The effects of hypoxia can occur at low altitudes.		
Hyperventilation is when your body expels too much oxygen.		
Carbon monoxide poisoning is a real concern for pilots while flying.		
Ear blocks are more painful when climbing than descending.		
A somatogravic illusion is due to slow bank.		
The parts of your eyes that you use at night are called the cones.		

LESSON 7

CHAPTER 13 EXAM

ACTIVITY 1: Article Response and Rubric

Article Response

Write a one-paragraph response that includes a summary and reflection on the following prompts:

1. Describe your thoughts on seeing how the air travel changed in China, the Middle East, and Europe prior to March 24.

2. When watching the animation of air travel over the United States, why does there appear to be a gap in the flights between Indianapolis and the District of Columbia?

3. Describe your thoughts on reading about the financial impact of COVID-19 on the airlines.

4. Describe your thoughts when seeing the pictures of the numerous airports where airplanes are parked across the world.

Include at least two thoughtful, inquiry-related questions in your reflection. Your response will be graded using the rubric provided on the next page.

_____

_____

_____

_____

_____

_____

_____

_____

_____

_____

_____

_____

_____

_____

RESPONSE RUBRIC

	Exceeds Expectation (4)	Proficient (3)	Partially Proficient (2)	Novice (1)	Non-Performance (0)
Summary	Information is clearly summarized and demonstrates understanding of the topic. Includes strong supporting details addressing the who, what, where, when, why, and how questions.	Information from source is summarized and general comprehension is demonstrated. Includes supporting details addressing the who, what, where, when, why, and how questions.	Summary may be unclear, incomplete, copies the article, or is inaccurate. There is a need for more supporting details. Summary is only a few sentences.	Summary is vague, too much information was copied from the article, or important details are left out. Details or summary may be confusing.	No summary included.
Reflection	Student is able to relate article content to class material. Insightfully gives personal response with extremely strong thoughts and ideas. Two thoughtful, inquiry related questions are present.	General connection made between article and class material. Tells what their thoughts of the article are, with detail and description. Attempts to push thinking with some prompts. Two questions are submitted that relate to the field of aviation.	Simple or brief connection made between article and class material. Attempts to tell what their thoughts about the article. Lacks thoughtful ideas that relate to the article. Only one question present and/or are not applicable.	Attempt made to relate article content to class material. Response is inappropriate to the content of the article. Questions attempted.	No response written.
Conventions	Writer makes little or no errors in grammar or spelling that distract the reader from the content. Paragraphs contain sentences that are well-constructed. There are varied beginnings and rich and appropriate vocabulary.	Writer makes very few errors in grammar or spelling that distract the reader from the content. Most sentences are well-constructed with varied beginnings and vocabulary.	Writer makes some major errors in grammar or spelling. Some sentences may not be well-constructed. Similar words are used too often.	Writer makes many errors in grammar or spelling. Sentences lack structure and appear incomplete or are confusing.	No writing submitted or is illegible.

Comments

Total _____ / 12 pts

CHAPTER 14

NAVIGATION AND CROSS-COUNTRY FLIGHT PLANNING

CONTENTS

Check off each activity upon completion.

LESSON 1

E6B INTRODUCTION

ACTIVITY 1: Using an E6B Flight Computer

Time, Speed, Distance Problems:

$$\frac{\text{SET MPH (KTS)}}{\blacktriangle} = \frac{\text{DIST. (OUTER)}}{\text{TIME (INNER)}}$$

Fill in the answers completed by the facilitator. Complete the remaining questions as assigned by the facilitator.

1. Rate: 80 kts   Distance: 100 NM   Time: _____ min

2. Rate: 75 km/h   Distance: 40 km   Time: _____ min

3. Rate: 80 mph   Distance: _____ SM   Time: 15 min

4. Rate: 65 kts   Distance: _____ NM   Time: 90 min

5. Rate: _____ kts   Distance: 25 NM   Time: 10 min

6. Rate: _____ kts   Distance: 60 NM   Time: 35 min

Fuel Consumption Problems:

$$\frac{\text{SET GAL./HR.}}{\blacktriangle} = \frac{\text{TOTAL GAL. (OUTER)}}{\text{TIME (INNER)}}$$

7. Rate: 15 GPH   Gallons: 9 gallons   Time: _____ min

8. Rate: 11.5 GPH   Gallons: 40 gallons   Time: _____ min

9. Rate: 8 GPH   Gallons: _____   Time: 90 min

10. Rate: 25 GPH   Gallons: _____   Time: 35 min

11. Rate: _____ GPH   Gallons: 3.5 gallons   Time: 14 min

12. Rate: _____ GPH   Gallons: 8 gallons   Time: 50 min

Wind Correction Angle (WCA) and Ground Speed:

13. TC: 235°   TAS: 95 kts   Wind: 180°@25 kts   WCA: _____ GS: _____ kts

14. TC: 176°   TAS: 85 kts   Wind: 160°@15 kts   WCA: _____ GS: _____ kts

15. TC: 203°   TAS: 115 kts   Wind: 350°@17 kts   WCA: _____ GS: _____ kts

Density Altitude (DA):

16. PA: 1,800 ft   Temp: 20°C   DA: _____ ft

17. PA: 5,700 ft   Temp: −35°C   DA: _____ ft

18. PA: 3,500 ft   Temp: −05°C   DA: _____ ft

19. PA: 7,500 ft   Temp: 15°C   DA: _____ ft

LESSON 2

CONSIDERATIONS FOR PLANNING A CROSS-COUNTRY

ACTIVITY 1: Factors to Consider When Planning a Cross-Country

Part A—Considerations

Write down at least five considerations that must be taken into account to safely fly a cross-country flight.

1. _____

   _____

2. _____

   _____

3. _____

   _____

4. _____

   _____

5. _____

   _____

Part B—Additional Considerations

Compare your results with those on the board. What are three additional considerations you did not think of that you now see as important?

1. _____

   _____

2. _____

   _____

3. _____

   _____

Part C—Two-Column Graphic Organizer

Looking at your weather—Summarize the weather conditions and other key factors you have researched and been briefed on by classmates This information will also be used as you plan your cross-country.

1. METAR for along route, departure and arrival airports	
2. TAF for along route, departure and arrival airports	
3. Prognostic charts	
4. Convective activity	
5. Winds and temperature aloft forecast	
6. NOTAMs for your departure and arrival airport	
7. Are there hangars, parking, and lodging available at your destination airport?	
8. Are fuel services available at your destination airport?	
9. Are there maintenance services available at your destination?	

Part D—Making a Go/No-Go Decision

Complete the following sentence by circling GO or NO-GO:

1. Based on the weather and other important factors discussed, I would **(GO or NO-GO)** on this flight.

_____

Depending on your answer to question #1:

2. Explain your decision to GO or NO-GO on this flight.

_____

_____

_____

_____

_____

_____

_____

_____

_____

_____

_____

LESSON 3

INTRODUCTION TO NAVIGATION AND USING PILOTAGE

ACTIVITY 1: Navigation Log

(See next page.)

ACTIVITY 2: Pilotage and Navigation Quiz

1. List the three forms of navigation used by pilots and explain each of them.

_____

_____

_____

_____

_____

_____

_____

_____

2. What are two things that make a checkpoint "good"?

_____

_____

_____

Find an example on your sectional of a good checkpoint for each the conditions described in Questions 3–7.

3. A clear day flying at 4,500 feet above the ground.

_____

_____

_____

4. If you are flying very close to the ground, such as 500 feet or 1,000 feet above the surface.

_____

_____

_____

(continued on page 350)

Flight Planner

asa

Preflight

PLANNED			PREDICTED WIND		TEMP	PLAN TAS	WIND CORR ANGLE -L +R	TRUE HEADING -E +W VAR	MAG HEADING ± DEV
TRUE COURSE	ALTITUDE		DIRECTION	VELOCITY					

AIRCRAFT	N	TIME OFF	BLOCK START	BLOCK END
ATIS CODE		SKY	TEMP	WIND
		ALTIMETER	RUNWAY	EST GPH

En Route

Checkpoints	COMPASS HEADING	DIST LEG REM	GS EST ACT	ETE ATE	ETA ATA	FUEL USED FUEL REM.	VOR FREQ IDENT	BEARING TO/FROM	TRANS-PONDER CODES "SQUAWKS"
DEPARTURE									
ARRIVAL									
TOTALS									

Terminal Information

Field	Elevation	Runways	Radio Frequencies

Notes:

ASA-FP-3

5. If you are flying at night.

_____

_____

_____

6. If you are flying 10,000 feet above the surface.

_____

_____

7. If you are flying with visibility less than 4 NM.

_____

_____

LESSON 4
DEAD RECKONING

ACTIVITY 1: Navigation Logs

(See next page.)

ACTIVITY 2: Definitions and Terms

Record the definitions of these terms that are found in the *Pilot's Handbook of Aeronautical Knowledge.*

- True course (TC) _____

_____

_____

- True heading (TH) _____

_____

_____

- Magnetic course (MC) _____

_____

_____

- Magnetic heading (MH) _____

_____

_____

- Wind correction _____

_____

_____

- Compass deviation _____

_____

_____

(continued on page 353)

Flight Planner — Preflight

TRUE COURSE	PLANNED ALTITUDE	PREDICTED WIND DIRECTION	VELOCITY	TEMP	PLAN TAS	WIND CORR ANGLE -L +R	TRUE HEADING	VAR -E +W	MAG HEADING	± DEV	En Route Checkpoints	COMPASS HEADING	DIST LEG	DIST REM	GS EST	GS ACT	ETE	ATE	ETA	ATA	FUEL USED	FUEL REM	VOR FREQ	VOR IDENT	BEARING TO/FROM	TRANSPONDER CODES "SQUAWKS"
84	3500 ↗	330	6	16°C	76	-4	80	-12	68	+2	**DEPARTURE** KMYF	70	8		78		06:09		14:06		0.8					1200
														85								42.2				
68	1500	305	20	8°	76	-13	55	-12	43	+2	Gillespie	45	10		85		07:04		14:13		0.9					
														75								41.3				
34	1500	305	20	8°	110	-11	23	-12	11	+1	El Cap Reservoir	12	18		108		10:00		14:23		1.3		114.0		22 TO	
														57								40				
33	1500	305	20	8°	110	-11	23	-12	11	+1	Julian VOR	12	36		108		20:00		14:43		2.7		114.0		21 FROM	
														21								37.3				
304	1500 ↙	305	20	8°	110	0	304	-12	292	-1	Cochran	291	21		90		14:00		14:57		1.9		116.2		292 FROM	
														0								35.4				
											KPSP															
											ARRIVAL	**TOTALS**	93													

Header: AIRCRAFT N19630 · ATIS CODE Bravo · TIME OFF · SKY 10,000 Sc+ · ALTIMETER 29.92 · BLOCK START 1400 · TEMP · RUNWAY · WIND 23 · EST GPH 28 · BLOCK END

Terminal Information

Field	Elevation	Runways
KMYF	427	10L/R 28L/R
KPSP	476	13L/R 3L/R

Radio Frequencies

KMYF (G) 118.22 (T) 119.2

KPSP ATIS – 118.25 (G) 121.9 (T) 119.7

Notes:

KPSP – TPA 1,500 msl

Runway 13R/3lL 10,000 × 150 ft.

Runway 13L/3lR 4,952 × 75 ft.

ASA-FP-3

- Compass heading (CH) _____
  _____
  _____

- Magnetic variation _____
  _____
  _____

- Isogonic lines _____
  _____
  _____

- Agonic lines _____
  _____
  _____

ACTIVITY 3: Radio Navigation Practice

Route of flight: _____ to _____

What is the true course? _____

What is the magnetic course at your departure airport? _____

What is the magnetic course at your arrival airport? _____

LESSON 5

RADIO NAVIGATION

ACTIVITY 1: VOR Practice Problems

Use the pictures to determine the aircraft's location in relation to the VOR.

1. Where are you in relation to the VOR station? _____

2. Where are you in relation to the VOR station? _____

3. Where are you in relation to the VOR station? _____

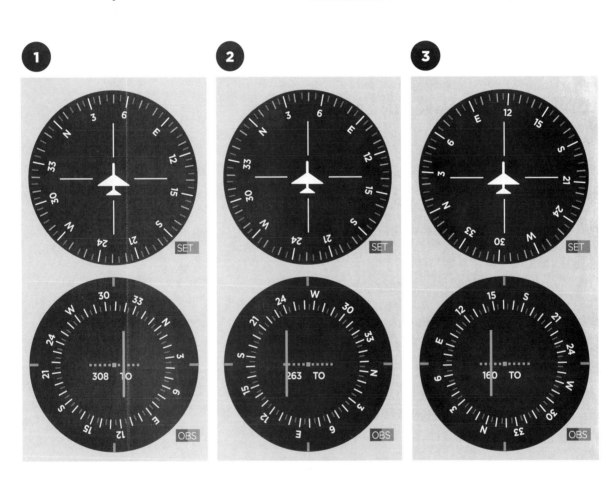

ACTIVITY 2: Radio Navigation Homework Problems

In preparation for your Cross-Country Planning lesson, review by completing the following questions.

1. While en route on a cross-country, you take your time between two checkpoints that are 15 NM apart. It takes you 12 minutes to travel between them. What is your ground speed in nautical miles per hour?

   _____

   _____

   _____

   _____

2. While planning for your cross-country, you want to see if you will have enough fuel to make it to your destination. Your aircraft burns 9 gallons per hour and you planned for your flight to take 3 hours and 20 minutes. How much fuel will it take to complete this flight?

   _____

   _____

   _____

   _____

3. If your aircraft burns 17 gallons per hour, how much fuel will you need to meet the VFR day reserves for the FARs?

   _____

   _____

   _____

   _____

4. You have calculated that your pressure altitude is 8,500 feet and 50°F. What is your density altitude?

   _____

   _____

   _____

   _____

LESSON 6

CROSS-COUNTRY PLANNING

ACTIVITY 1: Weight and Balance

	Weight	Arm	Moment
Basic Empty Weight (BEW)			
Pilot			
Front Passenger			
Rear Passengers			
Baggage			
Fuel			
Ramp Weight			
Run-up			
Takeoff Weight			

1. Are you within limits?

   _____

2. How much gas are you able to carry?

   _____

3. Do you have enough gas to make it to your destination based on whatever performance you plan to use for the flight (for example, 75% Best Power)?

   _____

   a. Do you need to plan a fuel stop?

   _____

ACTIVITY 2: Navigation Log

(See next page.)

Flight Planner

asa

Preflight

PLANNED				PREDICTED WIND		TEMP	PLAN TAS	WIND CORR ANGLE -L +R	TRUE HEADING +W -E	VAR	MAG HEADING ± DEV
TRUE COURSE	ALTITUDE			DIRECTION	VELOCITY						

En Route

AIRCRAFT	N	TIME OFF		BLOCK START		BLOCK END	
ATIS CODE		SKY		TEMP		WIND	

Checkpoints

DEPARTURE		COMPASS HEADING	DIST	GS	RUNWAY	ALTIMETER	ETE	ETA	FUEL USED	EST GPH	VOR			TRANS-PONDER CODES "SQUAWKS"
			LEG / REM	EST / ACT			ATE / ATA		FUEL REM.		FREQ / IDENT	BEARING	TO/FROM	

| ARRIVAL | | | TOTALS | | | | | | | | | | | |

Terminal Information

Field	Elevation	Runways	Radio Frequencies

Notes:

ASA-FP-3

© 1989–2019 Aviation Supplies and Academics, Inc.

ACTIVITY 3: Takeoff and Landing Distances

Takeoff ground roll: _____

Takeoff distance over a 50-foot barrier: _____

Landing ground roll: _____

Landing distance over a 50-foot barrier: _____

ACTIVITY 4: Two-Column Graphic Organizer

Looking at your weather—Summarize the weather conditions you have researched.

1. METAR for along route, departure and arrival airports	
2. TAF for along route, departure and arrival airports	
3. Prognostic charts	
4. Convective activity	
5. Winds and temperature aloft forecast	
6. NOTAMs for your departure and arrival airport	
7. Are there hangars, parking, and lodging available at your destination airport?	

8. Are fuel services available at your destination airport?	
9. Are there maintenance services available at your destination?	

ACTIVITY 5: Cross-Country Checklist

Put a checkmark by the following information verifying that it is filled out on your navigation log.

Information	Completed
1. Frequencies	
2. Airport diagram	
3. Departure field elevation	
4. Checkpoints (all of them along your route of flight)	
5. Navigation aids, identification and frequency	
6. Course, OBS	
7. True course	
8. Magnetic variation	
9. Distance, total and between checkpoints	
10. Altitude	
11. Ground speed	
12. Wind correction angle	
13. Estimated time en route	

LESSON 7

CROSS-COUNTRY SCENARIO

ACTIVITY 1: Filing a Flight Plan

Using the navigation logs from Lesson 6, fill out the flight plan on the following page.

Identify three variables that could arise at the last minute that might change your planning.

1. _____

   _____

2. _____

   _____

3. _____

   _____

International Flight Plan

U.S. Department of Transportation
Federal Aviation Administration

PRIORITY   ADDRESSEE(S)

<=FF

FILING TIME   ORIGINATOR   **<=**

SPECIFIC IDENTIFICATION OF ADDRESSEE(S) AND / OR ORIGINATOR

3 MESSAGE TYPE   7 AIRCRAFT IDENTIFICATION   8 FLIGHT RULES   TYPE OF FLIGHT

<=(FPL   —   —   —   **<=**

9 NUMBER   TYPE OF AIRCRAFT   WAKE TURBULENCE CAT.   10 EQUIPMENT

—   /   —   /   **<=**

13 DEPARTURE AERODROME   TIME

—   **<=**

15 CRUISING SPEED   LEVEL   ROUTE

—

<=

TOTAL EET

16 DESTINATION AERODROME   HR   MIN   ALTN AERODROME   2ND ALTN AERODROME   **<=**

18 OTHER INFORMATION

—

<=

SUPPLEMENTARY INFORMATION (NOT TO BE TRANSMITTED IN FPL MESSAGES)

19   ENDURANCE   EMERGENCY RADIO
          HR   MIN   PERSONS ON BOARD   UHF   VHF   ELT

—E/   **P/**   **R/** U   V   E

SURVIVAL EQUIPMENT   JACKETS
          POLAR DESERT MARITIME JUNGLE   LIGHT FLUORES UHF   VHF

          / P   D   M   J   / L   F   U   V

DINGHIES
NUMBER CAPACITY COVER   COLOR

D /   C   **<=**

AIRCRAFT COLOR AND MARKINGS

A/

REMARKS

N /   **<=**

PILOT-IN-COMMAND

C/   **)<=**

FILED BY   ACCEPTED BY   ADDITIONAL INFORMATION

NOTE: File and close flight plans at www.1800wxbrief.com, www.duats.com, or call 1-800-WX-BRIEF.
VFR pilots: remember to close your flight plan.